Ang[...]'T

and

Devils CAN'T

A Guide to Victory

---

by

Dr. Arman Stephens

McDougal Publishing is a ministry of The McDougal Foundation, Inc., a Maryland nonprofit corporation dedicated to
spreading the Gospel of the Lord Jesus Christ to as many people
as possible in the shortest time possible.

Published by:

McDougal Publishing
P.O. Box 3595
Hagerstown, MD   21742-3595
www.mcdougalpublishing.com

ISBN 1-58158-015-0

Printed in the United States of America
For Worldwide Distribution

Nay, in all these things we are more than conquerors through him that loved us. For I am persuaded, that neither death, nor life, nor angels, nor principalities, nor powers, nor things present, nor things to come, nor height, nor depth, nor any other creature, shall be able to separate us from the love of God, which is in Christ Jesus our Lord.

Romans 8:37-39

Dedication

To the loving memory of my father, **DR. W.K. STEPHENS**, who continually demonstrated the victorious life in Christ. No matter what the circumstances, he showed me that in all things we are more than conquerors through Jesus Christ. He showed me that nothing could separate us from the love of God. *Angels Won't and Devils Can't* if we understand who we are in Jesus. His faith and steadfastness were an inspiration to me.

Thanks, Dad.

Contents

Foreword by Ruth Ward Heflin

From the moment I met Pastor Arman Stephens, there was a special bonding in the Spirit. He is a man who looks victorious. He has experienced the victory of God in his own life, and in this book, *Angels Won't and Devils Can't,* he passes along to you the secrets he has learned through years of fasting and prayer, study of the Word of God and seeking God's face. It is these things that have brought him into a realm of total victory in God. We are always interested in reading the works of those whose lives have proven their teachings, and this man's life does just that.

Pastor Stephens has known many of these truths for years, but he himself and his ministry are coming to the forefront in this day in which God is revealing Himself in signs and wonders and miracles. Each time I have seen him recently, I have been blessed by his lovely Christ-like spirit and the fact that he always has gold dust on his face. His joy and delight in being a carrier of the glory of these last days is refreshing.

Ruth Ward Heflin
Ashland, Virginia

Foreword by Bob Shattles

I first met Pastor Arman Stephens at Rev. Ruth Ward Heflin's 1999 Men's Convention. He is indeed a wholehearted pursuer of God's glory. He presses in with real faith, and he fully expects to receive all that God has for him. He is not willing for anything to stand in the way of his receiving from the Lord. Consequently, he is consistently in a mode of self-examination and personal repentance, *"in order that times of refreshing may come from the presence of the Lord"* (Acts 3:19, NAS).

Like all of us, Pastor Stephens is faced with attempts by the enemy to block his progress in the anointing, but God has given him an unusual gift of depth in the Word. This gift has brought him victory.

Angels Won't and Devils Can't will be a very valuable tool for all those who will read it and learn from it. As this pastor reveals the scriptural process of being an overcomer, your soul will be thrilled. He will show you how to experience victory after victory on your way to obtaining and walking in the awesome glory of our Lord.

I wholeheartedly recommend this book as a MUST for all who would desire to receive more of God's glory, either in their personal lives or in their ministries. You and everyone around you will be blessed by what you learn here. Blessing after blessing will pour out of Heaven upon you in the form of a glorious anointing.

I have been in Pastor Stephens' church for "Fire and Glory" meetings and witnessed many salvations, healings and deliverances, as the glory of God fell like a golden rain on us all. You can have the same experience as you follow the way that he has gone. You can receive your own victories!

Bob Shattles
Pastor, evangelist
Author of Revival Fire and Glory
and Souls Harvest

Introduction

Angels Won't and Devils Can't separate us from the love of God, and men don't have the power to do so either. That's why we can say with Paul, *"Thanks be unto God, which always causeth us to triumph in Christ"* (2 Corinthians 2:14)!

I know what it is to be defeated, and what I have written has been learned through personal experience. I thank God that I now have the victory, and I know that there is no way the devil can get me down or drag me under again.

There is absolutely nothing the devil can do about my victory, as long as I walk in obedience to the commandment of God's Word. There is no devil in Hell that has power to separate me from God. I am the only one with the power to relinquish His love.

Having gained such victory in my own life, I have a great desire to see other members of the Body of Christ walk and live in the blessings that already belong to them in Christ. Because of the overwhelming victory that Christ won for us through God's great plan of redemption, we have certain rights, blessings and benefits. We *have* victory! It already belongs to us. Jesus Christ came to Earth and fulfilled God's plan so that we could experience that victory and live overcoming lives. His will is that we overcome sin, sickness, poverty and spiritual death.

What Christ did for us is so real that we can experience the reality of His victory in our everyday lives. That is the purpose of this book. I want to help believers everywhere understand the will of God for their lives. I want every believer to know that he or she can walk in complete victory over the enemy and over the tests and storms of life that come against us all. I am not content that this victory be a theory. My desire is that every believer realize this victory personally.

Satan is a clever thief who has blinded us to many truths. He is a serious foe. But the good news is that Satan is defeated. Christ defeated Satan in His death, burial and resurrection, and He took from him the keys of death, Hell and the grave.

Armed with this knowledge, you, as a believer, can effectively overcome tests and trials and win in the battle of life. I promise that *Angels Won't and Devils Can't* keep you from it, and by the time you finish reading these pages, you will know it too!

Arman Stephens
Oklahoma City, Oklahoma

1

Victory, a Way of Life

*Now thanks be unto God, which
always causeth us to triumph in
Christ, and maketh manifest the
savour of his knowledge by us
in every place.*
2 Corinthians 2:14

Victory is God's standard for His children, and because of that, it is shocking
to see the way many Christians are living today. Literally thousands of
Christian men and women are living
in a subnormal status — as far as God
is concerned.

11

I'm not talking about unbelievers. I'm talking about people who have accepted Jesus Christ as their Lord and Savior, people who are born again, love the Lord and are members of a local church. These people are members of the Body of Christ, yet when you talk to them about a continual, perpetual victory, they look at you as though they don't know what you're talking about.

You may be guilty yourself of making the frequently heard statement, "I know it's possible to be victorious, but I don't think there is anyone who is really living in constant victory every day." I beg to differ. The divine standard of God, according to His Word, is total, continuous, overcoming victory.

Victory is the only state that God intends for His people. Victory is His divine order and plan for our lives. We should be experiencing victory every day.

I must admit that I haven't lived in perfect victory all of my life, and I am sure that you probably haven't either. Through Christ, however, we all have the potential for experiencing victory and seeing great changes take place in our lives. We need not live with victory one day and defeat the next — up today and down tomorrow — when God's standard is to *always* cause us to triumph in Christ Jesus.

We must reach a place in our Christian lives where we stop going up and down, and we start living in the constant state of victory God has planned for us. God's measure is for us always to triumph in every place so that the savor of His knowledge might be made manifest in our lives. Let's step into that plan.

I want to convince you beyond a shadow of a doubt that it is God's plan for you to live in victory *all* the time. God has given us great promises concerning victory. The apostle Paul wrote:

> *But thanks be to God, which giveth us the victory through our Lord Jesus Christ.*
> 1 Corinthians 15:57

The first promise we examined, in 2 Corinthians 2:14, deals with the time and place of victory. The time is *"ALWAYS"* and the place is *"EVERY PLACE."* This second promise, in 1 Corinthians 15:57, shows us that victory is ours as a *gift* from God through Jesus Christ. In other words, victory is yours to receive and enjoy!

John wrote to the churches:

> *For whatsoever is born of God overcometh the world: and this is the victory that overcometh the world, even our faith. Who is he that overcometh the world, but he that believeth that Jesus is the Son of God?*   1 John 5:4-5

Believing Is Having

The essential condition for receiving victory is to believe that Jesus is the Son of God. If we believe on Him, we have victory. If we believe that God is, and that He is a rewarder of them that diligently seek Him (see Hebrews 11:6), we have victory. If we believe that we have received everlasting life through Jesus Christ and have received Him as our Lord, we have received the gift of victory. That is a sure thing, and we can say with assurance: *Angels Won't and Devils Can't* take it from us!

We, however, must do our part, and our part is simply to believe. As John showed the believers of the early Church, the requirement for walking in this victory is faith. If you believe, you will have victory. It's there for the taking.

Victory is not something that the Christian moves into after a long, hard battle with the enemy. Victory is not some prize that we may perhaps someday obtain. We *already possess* victory. It's already ours! Victory and faith are one and the same; there is no separation of the two. You cannot take faith away from victory or victory away from faith. If you have faith, you have victory; and if you have victory, you have faith. The two go hand-in-hand. *"THIS is the victory that overcometh the world, EVEN OUR FAITH."*

You can no more separate faith from victory than

you can separate the sun from light. You can no more separate victory from faith than you can separate the guilty conscience from sin. If you have one, you have the other. If there is a fountain, there is water springing up. If there is no water, then there is no real fountain. If there is a mirror reflection, then there must be a mirror that causes that reflection. If there is no true reflection, then the "mirror" may be only a piece of glass. You cannot separate one from the other, and neither can you separate faith from victory.

What is this faith that cannot be separated from victory? It's the faith spoken of by Mark when he wrote:

> *And Jesus answering saith unto them, Have faith in God. For verily I say unto you, That whosoever shall say unto this mountain, Be thou removed, and be thou cast into the sea; and shall not doubt in his heart, but shall believe that those things which he saith shall come to pass; he shall have whatsoever he saith.*
>
> Mark 11:22-23

There are two powerful sentiments expressed here: that all things are possible, and that we can have what we believe for. This is the victory and the faith of which we speak.

This faith is not in *our* ability, but in *God's* ability, for in the original Greek this passage reads, *"Have the faith of God."* God intends for us to live in victory.

Paul wrote to the church at Rome concerning victory:

> For if by one man's offence death reigned by one; much more they which receive abundance of grace and of the gift of righteousness shall reign in life by one, Jesus Christ.
>
> Roman 5:17

Paul traced the fact that sin, defeat and death came through the sin of one man, Adam. But, he said, a new Man had come — the Lord Jesus Christ — and by His righteousness came victory and faith.

When we come into Jesus Christ, we're no longer of the old man, Adam. We have become of the new Man, of Jesus Christ, and we have victory in Him.

The book of Romans explains that we have been baptized into Christ's body, and our life no longer stems from Adam, but from Christ Himself (see Romans 6:3-4). Was there ever a more victorious person on this Earth than the Almighty Son of God? Even though He was crucified, death didn't stop His victory. He arose from the grave, ascended to the right hand of the Father, and is ever living to make intercession for you and me.

You talk about victory! That's why Paul could say, when he had come to the end of his life:

> *O death, where is thy sting?*
> *O grave, where is thy victory?*
>   1 Corinthians 15:55

There is no other real victory than that which God gives to us!

Paul's Testimony of Victory

In his writings, Paul defiantly, yet triumphantly, laughed at death and defied *"principalities," "powers," "rulers of the darkness of this world"* and *"spiritual wickedness in high places"* (Ephesians 6:12). He faced these valiantly, hurling himself at those things and telling them that they had no power or authority over him.

Then Paul boldly declared that even if he were killed or tortured *"all the day long,"* victory still belonged to him (see Romans 8:36). He firmly contended that nothing could separate him from the love of God that he had in Christ Jesus — not tribulation, distress, angels, demons, principalities, powers, or things past, present or future. Nothing on this Earth could take away his victory (see Romans 8:35-39). Not only did Paul declare that he was a conqueror; he was, he said, *"more than [a] con-queror through [Jesus Christ]"* (verse 37).

This is perhaps Paul's strongest statement concerning the continual victory God has ordained for His children. This is the pattern we should see in the life of every born-again believer.

"More Than Conquerors" in Both Old and New Testaments

David was *"more than a conqueror"* when he slew Goliath. He not only killed the giant with one small stone, but he also cut off Goliath's head and raised it up for all the opposing army to see (see 1 Samuel 17:48-54). In this way, David proved that he had more than conquered his enemy! This is the victory and the overcoming life that I'm writing about.

Paul said that we *are* more than conquerors through Christ who loved us. We are — right now. We're not talking about having victory "one of these days." We're talking about living the overcoming, faith-filled life RIGHT HERE AND RIGHT NOW!

God's victory is sure, assured, complete and final. Because of its absolute certainty, some people lose sight of it and begin to think that it is unobtainable. It isn't.

Jesus proved this victory in His life when He turned one little boy's lunch into enough bread and fish to feed five thousand men (besides women and children who were present) (see Matthew 14:15-21, Mark 6:35-44, Luke 9:12-17 and John 6:5-13). Jesus didn't feed only one little boy. He provided more than enough food for some twenty thousand or more people. *That* is victory. *That* is being *"more than a conqueror"*!

Jesus talked of this same kind of victory when He told of the prodigal son. The lad had squandered his inheritance, yet he was received again by his father and restored into the family (see Luke 15:11-24). He was restored, but not just to his original privileges of sonship; his father went further than that. He placed a special ring on his finger, adorned him with special robes and had a feast prepared in his honor.

The disciples experienced this total victory when they were caught in the midst of a terrible storm on the Sea of Galilee. There was no hope in sight, yet when Jesus came walking on the water and stepped into their boat, not only did the winds cease and the waves become still, but the boat and its passengers were immediately transported to the point of their destination. This total victory in the Lord Jesus Christ is the kind of life that God wants you and me to live!

On another occasion, the disciples had fished all night and had caught nothing. Jesus told them to cast their net on the other side of the boat. Now, there is no reason to believe that one side of the boat was different from the other. The difference was that *God* was in the boat this time. When the disciples were obedient to Jesus' command, they pulled up a net-breaking load of fish (see Luke 5:1-6).

The same thing happened again after Jesus' resurrection. When the fish were brought to shore and counted, there were one hundred and fifty-three (see John 21:1-11).

Someone might ask, "Why one hundred and fifty-three?" The number 100 represents the hundredfold return God has promised for our giving. The number 50 represents the Day of Pentecost, and it is, therefore, symbolic of the power of the Holy Spirit in our lives. And the number 3 represents the Triune God!

Our Present Victory

The Pharisees believed themselves to be free and victorious, yet Jesus told them they were still in bondage. He did offer them a hope, though. He told them that if they would believe on Him, the Son of God, they would be made free. He said:

> *If the Son therefore shall make you free, ye shall be free indeed.*   John 8:36

When are we to become free? When are we to become victorious? Is it sometime in the future? Is it
only when Christ comes back for His Church and
takes us to Heaven? No. For us, victory must be a
present, everyday standard, or norm, for God has
given it to all of His children as part of our relationship with Him.

Several times throughout the New Testament, the
phrase "Grace and peace be multiplied to you" is
used. This is the victory that is ours. God always
multiplies His gifts and gives us more than enough.
Even as the stars of the heavens and the sands of
the seashore are too numerous to count, so are the
blessings of God's victory toward us.

Peter also wrote of this limitless victory:

> *Grace and peace be multiplied unto you through*
> *the knowledge of God, and of Jesus our Lord,*
> *according as his divine power hath given unto*
> *us all things that pertain unto life and godli-*
> *ness, through the knowledge of him that hath*
> *called us to glory and virtue: whereby are given*
> *unto us exceeding great and precious promises:*
> *that by these ye might be partakers of the di-*
> *vine nature, having escaped the corruption that*
> *is in the world through lust.*   2 Peter 1:2-4

Notice what he said in verse 4: *"Whereby are given*

unto us EXCEEDING GREAT and PRECIOUS promises." This word, *exceeding,* means "more than you
can count." The word translated *great* means "big-
ger than you could possibly imagine." And this
word, *precious,* means "something that is dear to
you." These are the promises of God that tell us we
have become partakers of His divine, victorious nature.

God has never lost a battle, nor a round in a fight.
He is *always* the Winner. Since we are partakers of
His divine nature, then we are always victorious. It
is written:

> *As he is, so are we in this world.*
>
> 1 John 4:17

We Were Born Again to Be Overcomers!

Paul wrote to the Roman believers:

> *For sin shall not have dominion over you: for*
> *ye are not under the law, but under grace.*
>
> Romans 6:14

Because you are not under the Law, but under
grace, and because sin has no dominion over you,
then *defeat* should not be part of your vocabulary.
Victory should be your norm for living.

God spoke to Paul and said:

*My grace is sufficient for thee: for my strength
is made perfect in weakness.*

2 Corinthians 12:9

When you feel weak and unable to go any further, remember that there is strength and victory in
Christ Jesus!

Are we to triumph only once in a while? Remember that Paul declared our victory to be *"ALWAYS."*
And what is this triumph, or victory, that God gives
us? It is our faith.

How about you? Have you been living victoriously, or have you been going through life with a
defeatist attitude? You don't have to be defeated,
because you were given the gift of victory when you
accepted Jesus as your Savior.

I know what it is to feel discouraged and defeated
at times, and I realize that Satan does come against
us to try to make us feel that way. But I also understand that defeat and discouragement are not God's
norm for us. God's standard for each of us is that
we never be defeated, but that we always triumph
and be victorious. This victory is not something we'll
obtain *someday*, but it is something we already *have*
if we have accepted Jesus Christ as Lord and Savior.

You will never receive any more victory than you

have right now. God has already given you complete victory. It's yours right now. You don't have
to wait until you get to Heaven. You won't have any
more problems there, so, of course, you will have
victory. But you can also enjoy victory right now —
today.

The apostle Paul did not say that we would never
be tempted or tested. He himself was persecuted,
run out of town, beaten, imprisoned, stoned and
shipwrecked. Through it all, however, he maintained his victory in Jesus. In the midst of all the
storms and problems that came against him, Paul
knew who he was in Christ. He was an overcomer
and more than a conqueror — and he lived like it!

2

Victory, a Present-Tense Reality

And from Jesus Christ, who is the faithful witness, and the first begotten of the dead, and the prince of the kings of the earth. Unto him that loved us, and washed us from our sins in his own blood, and hath made us kings and priests unto God and his Father; to him be glory and dominion for ever and ever. Amen.

Revelation 1:5-6

We need not wait to have victory

25

sometime in the future. We *already* have it. God provided it through Jesus' death, burial and resurrection, and when we accepted Jesus Christ as Savior and Lord, we obtained that victory.

John's revelation concurs with this truth. Notice that the verbs in this passage are in the past tense: *"Unto him that LOVED us, and WASHED us from our sins in his own blood, and HATH MADE us kings and priests unto God."* God has already done it.

For whom did He do it? *"[He] loved US, and washed US ... and made US kings and priests unto God."*

Our Faith Is Our Victory

How would you like to live in victory every single day of your life? If you are diligently seeking to enter into this state of perpetual victory, it is important that you realize and understand that this victory is already yours. Once you realize that, you enter in and experience that victory by faith. *"God [has] dealt to every man the measure of faith"* (Romans 12:3), and *"this is the victory that [overcomes] the world, even our faith"* (1 John 5:4).

So, this victorious life is not something that we must constantly strive for, or something that only a few people can obtain. Nor is victory something that God will add to us later in our Christian lives. Victory IS ALREADY OURS. It belongs to us NOW!

Every Christian receives this glorious victory by

inheritance when he receives Jesus Christ as Lord
and Savior, for the Bible says that we *"are complete
in him"* (Colossians 2:10) and have *"all things"*
(1 Corinthians 3:21). God has raised us up and has
made us *"sit together in heavenly places in Christ Jesus"*
(Ephesians 2:6). We have already received this blessing of victory.

Paul wrote to the Corinthians:

> *But of him are ye in Christ Jesus, who of God is
> made unto us wisdom, and righteousness, and
> sanctification, and redemption.*
> 1 Corinthians 1:30

These gifts — *"wisdom," "righteousness," "sanctification,"* and *"redemption"* — cannot be bestowed
upon us today or in the future any more than they
already were when we first came into the knowledge of Christ Jesus. God has already done it.

God doesn't bring you halfway into His grace in
the experience of Christianity. He brings you fully
into the life of Jesus Christ. You don't receive a *measure* of the grace of God; you receive the grace of
God in its *fullness.* You don't receive a *measure* of
the Holy Spirit — you receive the Holy Spirit in His
fullness! The key to experiencing this fullness is to
release, by faith, what God has already given you.

We are not brought into Jesus Christ one piece at
a time! We are brought into Him once and for all,

completely and totally. In a sense, the apostle Paul had no more of the fullness of Jesus Christ than someone has today who just received Jesus as Lord and Savior. It may *seem* as though Paul had more of the fullness of Christ, but he didn't. He just learned to use, or experience, what God had already given to him.

Scientists have reported that we utilize only five percent of our total brain capacity. Still, consider all the modern technology that has come from the use of that small portion of the brain. Obviouly, we have vast untapped potential.

Our brains are totally complete and available to us, but our use of them determines how much knowledge and understanding we will gain in life. The same principle applies to our Christian experience. When we receive Jesus Christ, we receive the Holy Spirit, but our spiritual growth and accomplishments are determined by the extent to which we use the ability and power of the Holy Spirit that was given to us.

One Christian does not receive more of Christ than another Christian; the "portion" of God that each one receives is the same. God doesn't look at one Christian differently than He looks at another. In fact, when God looks at us, He sees us in Jesus, for we are in Him. We have the same rights and privileges that Jesus has, for we are *"joint-heirs with [him]"* (Romans 8:17).

Jesus Was "Representative Man"

When Jesus came to Earth, He identified with man by becoming a "representative man" so that He could become our Substitute. If you have named Jesus Christ as your Lord and Savior, then everything that happened to Jesus happened to you as well.

When Jesus was crucified, we were crucified:

> *Our old man is crucified with [him].*
>
> Romans 6:6

As a Christian, you are dead to sin, for when *Jesus* died to sin, *you* died to sin. The proof of this is found in Paul's letter to the Colossians:

> *For ye are dead, and your life is hid with Christ in God.*   Colossians 3:3

When Jesus was buried in the tomb, we were buried also:

> *Therefore we are buried with him by baptism into death: that like as Christ was raised up from the dead by the glory of the Father, even so we also should walk in newness of life.*
>
> Romans 6:4

Jesus was raised up from the dead, and when God raised Him up, He raised us also from the dead:

> *[God] hath quickened us together with Christ,*
> *(by grace ye are saved;) and hath raised us up*
> *together.*   Ephesians 2:5-6

Jesus ascended to the Father to sit in His rightful position as the Son of God, and when He ascended, we did too:

> *And made us sit together in heavenly places in*
> *Christ Jesus.*   Ephesians 2:6

What happened to Jesus has happened to us. All that is His is ours. So, victory already belongs to you and me. If you have believed that He is the Son of God and that He has been raised from the dead, and if you have received Him as the Lord of your life, then you have within you the victory, power and grace of Jesus Christ.

Our Righteousness Comes From the Father

> *He that is joined unto the Lord is one spirit.*
>   1 Corinthians 6:17

Because not everyone has come to realize what our

legal standing in the Lord really means, we have not yet possessed all that is ours. We have not been "writing checks" on our heavenly bank accounts. Some have not experienced the victory that belongs to them because they are not sure of their personal standing before God. *"Jesus is different from me,"* they think. As Christians, however, we are *"one"* with the Father.

Most Christians have not yet fully grasped the meaning of the Savior's words when He said, *"The flesh profiteth nothing"* (John 6:63). Consequently, they have tried to stand on their own abilities and works to produce their own righteousness. The Word of God shows us that our own righteousness, the righteousness of man, is *"as filthy rags"* (Isaiah 64:6). In Christ, however, we become *"the righteousness of God"* (2 Corinthians 5:21).

Most Christians have not yet stood where Paul stood when he said:

> *For I know that in me (that is, in my flesh,) dwelleth no good thing.*   Romans 7:18

There's probably not a Christian alive on the Earth who would not wish to crucify sinful flesh and get rid of the "sinful self," or "bad self." Untold millions, however, experience failure after failure in their attempts to crucify the flesh. Why is that? I believe it is because they are trying to do it in themselves.

Most believers have not turned "self" completely over to God. They want to rule on the thrones of their lives, wearing their little tinsel crowns and acting like they're in control. They cannot be "in control" and still have victory, because there is no true righteousness apart from the righteousness of God. To control sinful flesh, we must take ourselves off the thrones and put Christ on the thrones of our lives. Unless He rules us, there will be no righteousness in our lives.

When Christ rules in a person's life, that person is not only rid of the "bad self," he is rid of the "good self" too. It is wrong for us to boast either of the good things we do or the bad things we do not do because our righteousness is from God alone.

There is a "bad self" and a "good self" within each of us, and although we are willing and even eager to be rid of the "bad self," many of us still hold on to the "good self." *I can handle this,* some think. *I have ability.* That's dangerous thinking.

When we encounter a problem and find that we cannot handle the situation, we call on God. "Oh, Lord, help me!" we pray, and that's good. The problem comes when God begins to work on the situation and we suddenly feel like we can "go it alone." We jump back into the situation and say, "Okay, Lord, I can take it from here." What a mistake that is! We need to get rid of the "good self," as well as the "bad self," and turn ourselves over to the Lord, assigning ourselves completely unto Him.

The person who hungers and thirsts after righteousness and this perpetual victory of God must realize that victory is not something that he has to seek after and work to obtain himself, but it is something that has already been given to him through Christ Jesus our Lord. You cannot have any more victory than you already have now — if you are in Christ.

If our problem is with understanding our legal standing in God, then we need to learn God's promises:

> *So then faith cometh by hearing, and hearing by the word of God.*   Romans 10:17

The more of the Word of God we get within us, the more faith we will have to live the overcoming, victorious life that already belongs to us.

Through the Word, we come to recognize the fact that we died to sin when we accepted Jesus as our Savior. We come to recognize that through His death on the cruel cross of Calvary, we died to sin with Him. It has already been done!

Dead to Sin and Alive Unto God

> *Likewise reckon ye also yourselves to be dead indeed unto sin, but alive unto God through Jesus Christ our Lord.*   Romans 6:11

What does this mean? This word translated *reckon* means "to believe and accept as fact — to consider it a reality." We are to *reckon* ourselves dead to sin and alive unto God. We are to *believe, accept and consider it a reality* that we are dead to sin and alive unto God. Our "selves" have become dead to sin, and we have become alive unto God.

Our reckoning of these facts does not produce them. To the contrary, our reckoning is based on the fact that these things have already happened. The same thing is true of our victory — the victory that has already been given to us. Our reckoning that we are victorious does not make us victorious. We reckon that we are victorious because victory has already been given to us.

In reckoning that we are victorious, we are simply agreeing with God. We are *believing, accepting* and *considering it a reality* that victory is ours. What a powerful truth!

Always Victorious

We know that victory is God's standard for His people. He *always* causes us to triumph. Constant and enduring victory seems like an unattainable goal to many. Some ask, "Do you mean to tell me that I can *always* be victorious?" Yes, I mean to tell you just that.

I am realizing more and more every day that victory is the standard God has ordained for His people. It is His will for our lives. His norm is not for us to be down in the dumps, to be discouraged. His norm is not for us to be on the mountaintop today and down in the valley tomorrow. The norm He has established for His people is that we live a consistent, steady, faith-filled, victorious, praising-the-Lord kind of life.

This is what God wants for us. The fact that many have not been willing to believe what He said about it is the reason that they have never reached that place of victory in their everyday lives.

Many people say, "If I confessed that I am always victorious, I would be telling a lie." God is not asking you to say something that is untrue. He would never ask you to lie. The fact is that you *have* been crucified with Christ. You *have* died with Him. You *have* been raised with Him. You *have* been made to sit in heavenly places in Christ Jesus. That's not a lie. It's the truth according to God's holy Word. If you haven't received it, that's not God's fault. He has provided it for you.

A Heavenly Point of View

Sometimes we tell people who are experiencing tests and trials, "Just keep looking up." According to God's Word, that's the opposite of what we should be doing. We need to look *down*, because God has *"made us sit together in heavenly places in Christ Jesus"* (Ephesians 2:6). We're not down, looking up. We're up with Christ, looking down. We are seated with Him, looking down on all the problems that come against us in the world. In Christ, we are above every one of those problems. We are sitting in heavenly places, rejoicing in the Lord, because no problems can get us down.

By looking down, I don't mean to say that we have the attitude "I don't care what's going on." I mean that we know that, regardless of what is going on, we are victors in Christ Jesus. He has given us the victory.

Many insist that in order to confess a truth like this one, they must confess it after the fact, and I don't disagree with that viewpoint. But this is a fact. The work is finished. Jesus did die, He was buried, and He was raised from the dead. We did die with Christ, we were raised with Him, and we have been made to sit in heavenly places with Him. This is a biblical fact. Nothing could be more certain. It has already been done, so we need to agree with God and confess it.

Such a confession is legitimate. It is "after the fact." It is based upon reality.

Some people say, "Well, I don't *feel* like confessing that. I don't *feel* victorious. I don't *feel* like anything good is happening in my life." But what you feel does not alter the facts of God's Word. The *fact* is that God has made us to sit in heavenly places with Him. The *fact* is that before the foundation of the world, Jesus was slain as the Lamb of God for sinners (see Revelation 13:8). In the foreknowledge of God, before this world ever came into existence, God set out His outline for the redemption of man. He left nothing to chance. It was done, and it was done well.

My friend, before you were ever born, God had already made provision for your salvation. His plan was completed when Jesus died on the cross some two thousand years ago. A person who was alive at the time of Jesus' crucifixion and resurrection could say, "I see it; therefore I believe it." However, our salvation had been an established fact in the mind of God long before. He knew it from the foundation of the world.

Your total redemption — your victory, your power, your overcoming life — is already a fact. It has already been accomplished. Your victory has nothing to do with whether you feel good or not. The *fact* is that Jesus died on the cross to redeem you from all your sins. The *fact* is that stripes were laid on His back so that you could be healed of all your sicknesses and diseases. The *fact* is that Jesus gave us power and dominion over all the creatures of the Earth.

These are already facts, so for you to confess, "I am healed, I am well," when you are not feeling well is not telling a lie. It is a confession of fact. You're not saying that you don't feel an ache or a pain. You're saying, "I believe that God has already done it for me through Jesus Christ. Therefore, I am healed. I am saved. I am the righteousness of God in Christ. I am victorious. I have peace in my life."

It's time that we get away from the negative concepts we have held of life. *Can't* and *won't* should not be part of our vocabulary. As born-again children of God, we have victory over circumstances.

The Power of the Tongue

Our words have the power to change the course of nature. James, in his letter to the churches, devoted an entire chapter to this all-important subject (James 3). Your words can change circumstances that may be depressing you and causing you to feel that everything is going wrong. By confessing the Word of God in faith, believing, you can turn things around.

You can even change weather patterns by your faith and confession. I had this experience when our new church was being built. We had to move out of the old building earlier than planned, and we began having services in the new building before the parking lot was paved. It had been raining off and on, and I knew that if it continued to rain, people wouldn't be able to park their cars on the lot. And if they had no place to park, they couldn't come to church and worship the Lord.

The Bible speaks of the power and authority we have through agreement:

> *If two of you shall agree on earth as touching any thing that they shall ask, it shall be done for them of my Father which is in heaven.*
> Matthew 18:19

I got another brother to agree with me in the name of Jesus that it would not rain on our property until we finished the paving. Rain might come in our direction, but it would go around us or over us, and none would touch our property. That was our confession.

We moved into the new building on a Saturday, and our first meeting there was to be the following morning. As we were moving, the sky began to cloud up. No sooner had we loaded our piano onto a pickup truck to take it to the new location than it began to rain.

"I thought you said it wasn't going to rain!" someone said to me. (I had "stuck my neck out" and told the entire church congregation that it would not be raining on our property.) In that moment, the Holy Spirit reminded me of my faith and confession. I had taken God at His word, and I was trusting Him to do a miracle.

We drove to the new church, and when we got close, we could see that the parking lot was completely dry. Not a drop of rain had fallen on our property. We have the power to change the course of the circumstances that affect our lives.

Some might say, "But you don't know *my* circumstances." "You don't know how bad things are" or "You don't realize 'this' or 'that.' " But it doesn't matter. We can change the circumstances of our lives and continue to walk in perfect victory. How can I say that? Because your total, complete victory has already been won in Christ. Now, it's just a matter of your confessing what God has already done.

You have victory. There's not a thing in your life that can defeat you if you'll recognize the fact that Jesus is the Lord of your life and that you have victory in Him. No matter how dismal things look or how dark the days seem, you have victory. It's not something you strive for. It's something that God has already given you as His child.

If you have not taken the steps necessary to become God's child, do it today. First, confess that you are a sinner in need of the Savior. Then, ask Jesus to come into your heart and life. Finally, confess that Jesus is Lord and that God has raised Him from the dead.

When you do this, believing what you have confessed, the Bible says that you will be saved:

> *That if thou shalt confess with thy mouth the*
> *Lord Jesus, and shalt believe in thine heart that*
> *God hath raised him from the dead, thou shalt*
> *be saved.*   Romans 10:9

If you have done this, you are now born again. Your sins have been forgiven, and you have received eternal life. Now, you will not go to Hell when you die; you will go to Heaven. You can expect to have *"peace that passeth understanding"* in your heart, and joy will flood your life. You will now have the righteousness of God and the Spirit of the Lord dwelling within you, and you can't get any closer to God than having Him living inside of you.

You can expect to have victory, for victory is for all those who have accepted Jesus Christ as Lord and Savior. You don't have to do anything for it. It's already been won by Jesus. His action in the past has made it a present-tense reality for you. Appropriate the victory that is yours by believing and confessing its truth in your life.

3

Victory and the Overcomer

To him that overcometh ...
Revelation 2:7, 17 and 3:21

In the second and third chapters of
the book of Revelation, we are given
a wonderful confirmation of the potential for victory for those who
accept it as the divine standard for
the believer. If you have not been living a victorious life, I want to show
you how to live in total victory all
the time, how to be an *overcomer.*

In these two chapters, the Lord is
speaking to the seven churches of

Asia. Seven is a perfect and complete number. Jesus wanted it understood that He was not speaking just to local groups of people. He was addressing all people of every generation and every place. By using this number, He signified that His instructions, exhortations and admonitions were for *everyone.*

I don't think there can be any doubt about this fact. As you read through His messages to the seven churches, you can easily see that the Redeemer was speaking to every man and woman, boy and girl, for He said:

> *He that hath an ear, let him hear what the Spirit saith unto the churches.*
> Revelation 2:7, 11, 17, 29, 3:6, 13 and 22

Jesus was in Heaven when He revealed Himself to John on the Isle of Patmos. He was speaking from the very throne of God to men and women everywhere. He was speaking to all churches in all lands throughout all ages, and He was telling them to be faithful and to live victorious, overcoming lives.

As I began to study this passage of scripture, I was struck by the fact that Jesus ended His message to each of the seven churches with a promise. The promises were varied, with different meanings for different groups.

To some, for instance, the Lord offered the privilege of partaking of the fruit of the tree of life. He talked about riches in glory, about power and about the forces that are marshaled to supply us with the blessings we need in our lives. These are blessings that every believer should have. Reading and understanding what God said in His letters to the seven churches almost leaves one breathless. I encourage each of you to read these two chapters for yourself, and I am confident that the promises they contain will thrill you.

All the promises of Revelation 2 and 3 have one thing in common: They are all made payable, so to speak, to one person, and that is the person who has learned the secret of victory, he or she who *"overcomes."* These wonderful promises can be claimed only by someone who has learned the secrets of victory in the Christian life.

Meeting the Conditions and Reaping the Promises

All the promises of God are based upon a condition (or conditions), and if we are willing to meet the condition(s), we can receive the promised benefits. Those who are unwilling to meet the condition(s) will not receive the benefits. If we want to walk in the victory described to the seven

churches of the book of Revelation, we must meet
the conditions attached to the promises given there.

The first promise, for instance, is:

> *He that hath an ear, let him hear what the Spirit*
> *saith unto the churches; To him that overcometh*
> *will I give to eat of the tree of life, which is in*
> *the midst of the paradise of God.*
>
> Revelation 2:7

God wants to give to His victorious ones the fruit
of the tree of life, and He is waiting for us to meet
the condition of overcoming. The same is true for
all the promises God gave to the churches of the
book of Revelation (and to us today).

The next promise was to the church at Smyrna:

> *He that hath an ear, let him hear what the Spirit*
> *saith unto the churches; He that overcometh*
> *shall not be hurt of the second death.*
>
> Revelation 2:11

The promise was that the believers of Smyrna
would *"not be hurt of the second death,"* meaning spiritual death. Again, the condition was that they
overcome.

The third letter and promise were written to the
church at Pergamos:

*He that hath an ear, let him hear what the Spirit
saith unto the churches; To him that overcometh
will I give to eat of the hidden manna, and will
give him a white stone, and in the stone a new
name written, which no man knoweth saving
he that receiveth it.*   Revelation 2:17

The promise here was that the believers of
Pergamos would be permitted to *"eat of the hidden
manna"* and would be given *"a white stone"* with *"a
new name"* written in it that *"no man knoweth saving
he that receiveth it."* Again, the condition for the
promise was that the believers of Pergamos
overcome.

The promise for the believers at Thyatira was that
they would be given *"power over the nations"*:

*And he that overcometh, and keepeth my works
unto the end, to him will I give power over the
nations.*   Revelation 2:26

Again, the condition was that they overcome and
keep the Lord's works *"unto the end."*

There was more to this promise to the church at
Thyatira. God promised them:

*And he shall rule them with a rod of iron; as
the vessels of a potter shall they be broken to*

*shivers: even as I received of my Father. And I
will give him the morning star.*

Revelation 2:27-28

To whom would all this blessing be given? To
those who *overcame*, to those who had learned to live
in victory.

The fifth letter was written to the church at Sardis.
The promise for them was that they would be
"clothed in white raiment," that their names would
not be blotted out of *"the book of life,"* and that Jesus
would confess their names before the Father and His
angels. As before, the condition was that they
overcome.

*He that overcometh, the same shall be clothed
in white raiment; and I will not blot out his
name out of the book of life, but I will confess
his name before my Father, and before his
angels.*   Revelation 3:5

The sixth letter was written to the church at Philadelphia. It contained a powerful promise:

*Him that overcometh will I make a pillar in the
temple of my God, and he shall go no more out:
and I will write upon him the name of my God,
and the name of the city of my God, which is*

> *new Jerusalem, which cometh down out of*
> *heaven from my God: and I will write upon him*
> *my new name.*   Revelation 3:12

As with each of the others, the promise to the believers of Philadelphia came with the condition that they overcome.

The seventh and final letter was written to the church at Laodicea. It contained what could be the most amazing promise of them all. We could even say that it is one of the greatest promises of the entire Bible:

> *To him that overcometh will I grant to sit with*
> *me in my throne, even as I also overcame, and*
> *am set down with my Father in his throne.*
>   Revelation 3:21

What a powerful promise! What could be greater than being with Jesus on His throne?

Still More Promises

Still, there is more to God's promises to the overcomer. The voice John heard said:

> *He that overcometh shall inherit all things; and*
> *I will be his God, and he shall be my son.*
>   Revelation 21:7

Surely there is not another scripture verse that more emphatically states God's will and desire for His children than this one. Nothing could top it. Christians simply must overcome. We have to do it. We have no choice in the matter. God's promises are laid up for those who overcome.

A little later in this chapter I will speak more of just how you can become an overcomer. You must do it, and you can. The Word of God declares it.

We are not just to be conquerors; we are to be *"more than conquerors."* In the same sense, we are not to almost overcome or barely overcome. We are to overcome in all things.

Each of the seven letters of Chapters 2 and 3, although addressed to an individual local church, was meant for every believer. To prove this, each one closed with those words, *"He that hath an ear, let him hear what the Spirit saith unto the churches."* May our ears be open to hear what God is saying to us. His message is clear. We are to be victorious and to overcome. We are to be *"more than conquerors"* through Christ Jesus who loved us.

Overcoming in the Gospels

Someone might ask, "If overcoming is so important, why didn't Jesus talk about it more when He was here on the Earth? Why don't the Gospels say much about this subject?" The answer is that the theme of the four gospels is primarily faith. No other requirement was made there. If we would believe, our faith would be sufficient to release the bounties of Heaven. Jesus Himself said that we would receive *"according to [our] faith"*:

> *According to your faith, be it unto you.*
> Matthew 9:29

In this passage, He had first asked a question (in verse 28), *"BELIEVE ye that I am able to do this?"* Then, in verse 29, He promised that if we could believe, we would receive.

Faith, Jesus said, was enough to make us whole:

> *Thy faith hath made thee whole.*
> Matthew 9:22, Mark 5:34, 10:52,
> Luke 8:48 and 17:19

Faith, Jesus said, was enough to save us:

> *Thy FAITH hath saved thee.*   Luke 18:42

Faith was a very important part of Jesus' message:

> *O thou of little FAITH, wherefore didst thou doubt?*   Matthew 14:31

> *And he [Jesus] could there do no mighty work,*
> *save that he laid his hands upon a few sick folk,*
> *and healed them. And he marvelled because of*
> *their unbelief [lack of faith].*   Mark 6:5-6

When Jesus was asked, *"What shall we do, that we might work the works of God?"* (John 6:28), He answered, *"This is the work of God, that ye BELIEVE on him whom he hath sent"* (verse 29).

Jesus also said:

> *He that BELIEVETH on me, as the scripture*
> *hath said, out of his belly shall flow rivers of*
> *living water.*   John 7:38

> *I am the bread of life: he that cometh to me shall*
> *never hunger; and he that BELIEVETH on me*
> *shall never thirst.*   John 6:35

Is there a conflict between the message of Jesus in the Gospels and His message in the book of Revelation? Is believing different from being an overcomer? Absolutely not. It is the same message.

Believing Is Overcoming

John's letter to the churches shows the connection between these two messages:

*For whatsoever is born of God overcometh the
world: and this is the victory that OVER-
COMETH the world, even our FAITH. Who
is he that OVERCOMETH the world, but he
that BELIEVETH that Jesus is the Son of God?*
1 John 5:4-5

There is no difference or conflict between faith and
overcoming. There is no conflict between believing
and experiencing victory. God does not demand one
thing in the Gospels and another thing in the book
of Revelation. In both sections of the Bible, God is
asking for one and the same thing. Faith and overcoming, or faith and victory, are interchangeable. If
you have faith that Jesus is the Son of God, then you
have victory. If you have victory, then you are believing that Jesus is the Son of God.

It follows logically that since faith and victory are
one and the same, then if we are not living victorious lives, there must be a lack somewhere in our
faith. If faith is in operation in our lives, then we are
victorious. So if we are not living victoriously, then
we need to examine our faith.

How can we do that? Well, we know how faith
comes to us:

*So then faith cometh by hearing, and hearing
by the word of God.*   Romans 10:17

The more of the Word of God you can get inside you, the greater will be your faith, and therefore, the greater your victory will be also. Every time we exercise our faith, we are victorious, but Paul described his faith as *"the faith of the Son of God"* (Galatians 2:20). God has given each of us His faith, and if His faith is operating in our lives, victorious things should be happening. The faith to overcome obstacles, therefore, comes from intimate contact with the Lord Jesus Christ. If you have not had a personal encounter with Jesus the Christ, then you cannot exercise faith in Him. Consequently, you cannot have victory in your life.

It is faith that seeks out the Lamb of God and trusts Him for cleansing. He then becomes, for us, the One who *"takes away the sins of the world."*

Exercise Faith to Receive What Belongs to You

When we believe on Jesus and receive Him as the Lord and Savior of our lives, something good begins to take place, and we receive the victory we need. We become washed and cleansed by the blood of Jesus. Our sins are remitted, and we become *"new creature[s]"* in Christ. *"Old things are passed away,"* and *"all things are become new"* (2 Corinthians 5:17). We are *"delivered from the power of darkness"* and *"translated into the kingdom of his [God's] dear Son"* (Colossians 1:13).

Once we begin to understand the fact that we are in Christ and He is in us, we will begin living with victory in sight in every area of our lives. We will understand that He has made us *"more than conquerors"* and has *"made us to sit in heavenly places with [Him]."* Once we understand that, we enter into a place of constant victory and we become victorious in everything we do.

Some Christians disagree. They say, "I can't be on the mountaintop all the time, you know." I'm not saying that we will never again experience tests, trials or temptations, but I am saying that even in the midst of the most terrible storm, we can still have victory in Jesus Christ. It doesn't matter if the weight of the whole world has pressed down hard upon you, you still have victory in Christ. And you can have it always — all the time.

When you come into this knowledge of victory in Christ Jesus, you can no more be defeated than Christ was defeated. If you realize who you are in Christ, if you realize what your rights and privileges are as a child of God, you cannot be defeated any more than Jesus Himself could have been defeated.

Turning What Seems Like Defeat Into Victory

Someone might say, "Didn't they nail Jesus to a

cross?" Yes, but He was not defeated. He rose up from the grave and ascended to the right hand of the Father, where He now makes intercession for you and me. And because He arose, we arose too, and we can have everlasting life.

Jesus was not defeated. Being nailed to the cross of Calvary may have looked like defeat for Him, but it wasn't. That was all part of God's plan to redeem us and reconcile us to Himself. He suffered Calvary for us.

Paul suffered many things in the flesh, but through it all, he knew what it was to walk in victory. Although he said that he was *"killed all the day long"* (Romans 8:36), *"persecuted"* and *"cast down,"* yet he declared that he was *"not forsaken"* (2 Corinthians 4:9).

It doesn't matter how many "hard knocks" you've had in life. It doesn't make any difference how many times you have been pushed down into the mire and filth of this world. If Christ is living in you, you cannot be defeated.

When the disciples were out on the Sea of Galilee and the storm came up, they feared for their lives. They thought their boat might sink with the force of the wind and the waves. If they had only known who was on board their ship, they would not have worried about the storm in the least. That ship could not go under, because Jesus was on board.

Your life cannot end in shipwreck, and you cannot go under if you really know the One living inside you.

We can no more go under or be conquered than Jesus Himself could. We have the promise of God:

Greater is he that is in you, than he that is in the world.   1 John 4:4

All things are possible to him that believeth.
Mark 9:23

Since we know that believing and overcoming are one and the same and we know the many promises made to the overcomer, we know that the believer should be one who overcomes. Faith and victory are inseparable.

If you are not living in victory, if you are not overcoming in life, it is undoubtedly because you are not exercising the faith of God. You can't blame your pastor, your spouse, your friend, your neighbor or anybody else for the defeat in your life. Victory is yours for the taking.

It's not that you don't have faith, for if you are a believer, God has dealt to you *"the measure of faith"* (Romans 12:3). You must begin to use the faith God has given you.

If you haven't been experiencing victory in your life, it may well be because you have not yet taken hold of God's Word or you haven't kept your eyes on Him. You've been looking at others instead, or you've been looking at your circumstances.

Choose to Believe the Greater Facts of God's Word

As we have seen, victory is not based on feeling. Some people want to feel that everything will be all right before they begin. Feeling will come, however, out of a fact, and the fact is that Jesus died some two thousand years ago to redeem you from your sins. The fact is that He was buried for you. He conquered death, Hell and the grave for you. He took stripes on His back so that you could be healed. He was raised from the dead, and He ascended to the right hand of the Father, where He ever lives to make intercession for you today.

Because of these facts, you and I have victory. God has made us to sit in heavenly places in Christ Jesus. We are overcomers and have victory because of who we are in Christ. Regardless of the circumstances that surround us or how badly we have been treated, we still have victory. Whether we have money or don't have money, we have victory.

I have found that as I exercise faith in God and

walk in the victory that He's already given me, all the things I need just keep coming to me. That's what God meant when He said:

> *He that overcometh shall inherit all things.*
>   Revelation 21:7

The desire of your heart is waiting for you. You have the victory if you know Jesus as your Lord and Savior. You have the faith to overcome and possess that which belongs to you in Him. Take it. It's yours!

4

Enemies of Your Victory

*The thief cometh not, but for
to steal, and to kill, and to
destroy.*   John 10:10

I am positive that we would not
need so much emphasis in the Scriptures on the need for victory in a
Christian's life if there were not
forces arrayed against the children of
God, working to keep us from victory. If there was not a battle going
on, if there was not a force trying to
destroy us and keep us from having
victory, there probably would not be

a whole lot said in the Scriptures about victory; it would be automatic.

Although the Savior calls us to an overcoming, victorious life, the Bible has much to say about the enemies of our victory. Although there is a strong emphasis on the promises and benefits of Heaven being offered to the overcomer, there are also many warnings about enemies who would rob us of those blessings.

Someone once described our life on this Earth by saying, "It is drawn sword all the way to Heaven." What he was trying to say is that from the time we get saved until we get to Heaven, there will be constant warfare trying to prevent our final victory with the Lord.

If you're not fighting a battle, it could be because you're not where the battle is. And if you're not where the battle is, it could be because you're not moving on with God in your Christian walk. All those who are serious about following the Lord and making Heaven their home will face many battles.

Facing battles is not a sign of spiritual lack. To the contrary, when I have found myself facing few spiritual battles, trials or temptations, it has usually been during periods when I prayed and studied God's Word the least. When I am in the Word of God and in prayer, seeking the Lord, things are happening in the spiritual realm, and *that* agitates Satan. It is then that the battle heats up.

From the time we give our lives to the Lord until the time we get to Heaven, we must have our swords drawn at all times. We must constantly rely on the Word of God as a tool against any enemy that would come against us.

There are many enemies that threaten our victory.

The Flesh

One of our greatest spiritual battles is not with the devil, but with our own flesh. Paul wrote to the Galatian church:

> *For the flesh lusteth against the Spirit, and the Spirit against the flesh: and these are contrary the one to the other: so that ye cannot do the things that ye would.* Galatians 5:17

There is a constant battle being waged in our lives between our flesh and the Spirit. If the flesh is in control and winning the battle over the Spirit, then we're in trouble. When we are ruled by the flesh, many hideous and ugly things are manifested in our lives. The Bible calls them *"the works of the flesh"*:

> *Now the works of the flesh are manifest, which are these; adultery, fornication, uncleanness,*

> *lasciviousness, idolatry, witchcraft, hatred,*
> *variance, emulations, wrath, strife, seditions,*
> *heresies, envyings, murders, drunkenness,*
> *revellings, and such like: of the which I tell you*
> *before, as I have also told you in time past, that*
> *they which do such things shall not inherit the*
> *kingdom of God.*   Galatians 5:19-21

When these manifestations have dominance in our everyday lives, it is easy to understand how they can quickly destroy our victory. So, flesh is one of the enemies that threaten to take away the victory that God has given to us through Jesus Christ.

Flesh does not always appear in obvious and loathsome ways. Sometimes it appears to be very legitimate and acceptable. Sometimes the flesh manifests itself in such a refined way that we don't even realize we are dealing with the lusts of the flesh.

But, however refined, our flesh is always at war with our spiritual side. It is *"at enmity"* with the Spirit.

The World

Although the first and worst enemy of our victory is our own flesh, another serious enemy is the world with all its pomp and greed. The world is full of lust for riches, for pleasure and for power. The world is determined to dominate our lives.

In the gospels, Jesus told the parable of the sower, in which He showed that one of the dangers to those who hear His Word is that *"the cares of this world"* and *"the deceitfulness of riches"* can *"choke"* out the growth of the good seed and make it unproductive (Matthew 13:22 and Mark 4:19).

When we have the Word of God in our lives, we have victory. That's why the things of this world try to choke out the effectiveness of the Word. Any time we begin to love the things of the world more than we love the things of God, this will choke out our victory, and anyone who is guilty of allowing it to happen is selling himself short.

Jesus said:

> *For where your treasure is, there will your heart be also.* Matthew 6:21 and Luke 12:34

We must never be so heavenly minded that we are no earthly good, but neither must we be so earthly minded that we are no heavenly good. There must be a balance in our lives so that, where the world is concerned, though we may be *in* it, the *world* is not in *us*. We are not to be tainted by the particular cares of this life, the deceitfulness of riches and the lust for other things. Those are the things of this world that can keep us from receiving the things of God. They are enemies of our victory.

Paul warned the Corinthians about the dangers of the carnal mind:

> *But the natural man receiveth not the things of the Spirit of God: for they are foolishness unto him: neither can he know them, because they are spiritually discerned.*
>
> 1 Corinthians 2:14

Our natural minds cannot understand *"the things of the Spirit."* When our minds are more "worldly concerned" than "heavenly concerned," it will be impossible for us to understand the things of God.

One of the reasons we are receiving such great revelation from the Word of God in these last days is that we have become more concerned with His Kingdom. Our minds have become more heavenly minded than worldly minded, and, therefore, we are able to receive more from God.

If your mind is tied to the things of the world, you are not free to receive heavenly revelation. If you are so burdened down with problems and cares of life that you have no time to pray and study the Word of God, then you will lose out in your spiritual life. The reason is that you will not be able to receive divine revelations from God. Such revelations come to those who allow themselves to be governed by the Spirit, and they are people of victory in Christ.

Those who are heavenly minded know that they have victory. They know that victory has already been given to them in Christ, and they are determined to walk in that victory. They will not allow the things of this world to taint their lives and destroy their effectiveness for the Kingdom of God.

Self

Aside from the flesh and the world, another great enemy of our victory, one of the subtlest, is *"self."* There is far too much self-love, self-esteem and self-confidence in those who call themselves Christians. Our sufficiency is in Christ, not in ourselves.

The Bible declares:

> *For I say, through the grace given unto me, to every man that is among you, not to think of himself more highly than he ought to think.*
> Romans 12:3

A few verses later, Paul added:

> *Be kindly affectioned one to another with brotherly love; IN HONOUR PREFERRING ONE ANOTHER.*   Romans 12:10

The philosophy of the world is totally opposite. It declares that you are "number one" and that you should take care of "number one" and let the rest of the world fend for itself.

It is not wrong to love yourself. If we do not love ourselves, we cannot properly love others. At the same time, we must love our neighbors as we love ourselves (see Leviticus 19:18, Matthew 19:19, 22:39, Mark 12:31, Luke 10:27, Romans 13:9, Galatians 5:14 and James 2:8). If we're not careful, self-love can dominate us to the point that the entire concern of our lives is the glory we ourselves will receive from whatever we are doing.

The key for the Christian is to love God first and self second, and we must come to love Him first if we are to walk in the fullness of our victory in Christ. This is totally contrary to our natural way of thinking. Throughout the ages, men have tried to make themselves the center of the universe and have maintained the attitude that the whole world revolves around them.

We must consider the possibility that there may be people on other planets. If that is possible, it is also possible that these other people have never sinned and therefore have never fallen as our race has. If that were true, they would be far superior to us.

Is this what Jesus meant when He said, *"Other*

sheep I have, which are not of this fold" (John 10:16)? Could He have been talking about other beings on other planets? If so, could this be the answer to the many U.F.O. sightings reported in recent years?

If beings who have never sinned do exist on other planets, then their knowledge would be vastly superior to ours, and they might have a capacity for interplanetary travel that is light years ahead of our own. I'm not saying that it is true, but I'm asking if it might be possible.

I say all this to emphasize the point that human beings in general have become so proud that they are certain the entire universe revolves around them. I am fully aware that God created man above everything else that is on this Earth and only *"a little lower than the angels"* (Psalm 8:5). It is evident that He intended for man to have dominion over everything else He created. But God did not give us this dominion so that we would lift ourselves up and think, *My, how great I am!* Yet that is the philosophy of the world today.

Many modern scientists are strongly of the opinion that what is in the mind of man is all that matters in this world. To their way of thinking, everything depends upon the human mind. This is a very enticing philosophy. We Christians must be careful not to get caught up in this kind of philosophy and not to be tricked into loving ourselves more than we love God.

Self-love is a deadly enemy of our victory because it can slip in in very subtle ways so that we don't even realize it's happening. How does this happen? For example, the members of some Christian denominations consider themselves to be superior to other Christians and think that they are the only ones who have the truth. This is dangerous self-delusion.

Jesus, recognizing the dangers of self, taught us:

> *If any man will come after me, let him deny himself, and take up his cross, and follow me.*
> Matthew 16:24

Both Mark and Luke record this important teaching as well (see Mark 8:34 and Luke 9:23). Jesus didn't ask us to deny some *thing;* He told us to deny *"self."* If we desire to follow Him, self-denial is required. Self must be put in subjection to God.

Again, most of us are willing to get rid of our "bad self," the one that is always in rebellion against God, but too often we want to hold on to our "good self." Paul, however, declared that there is no good thing in our flesh:

> *For I know that in me (that is, in my flesh,) dwelleth no good thing.*   Romans 7:18

"Self" must be subjected to death on the cross, and

once it is dead, we must keep it there. If we are going to walk, live and operate in the victory that God intends for us to have, the *flesh*, the *world* and *"self"* must be removed from our lives.

Satan, the Thief

A fourth enemy of our victory is the devil himself. Satan is very real, very much alive and very much at work on the Earth. One only needs to watch the evening news to know that this is true. There is no other explanation for why people would do such terrible things to each other than the fact that an evil force is influencing and driving them to do these things. There would not be so much hurt and sorrow in this world if there were not a being causing it.

The Word of God is very clear that God is love, and God is good. He is the Giver of all good things (see James 1:17). So how can we explain all the evil things happening on the Earth? There can be only one answer. There is another force at work in this world, and it is satanic. Satan is trying his best to destroy the victory in our lives. He hates God, and He knows that the best way to hurt God is to hurt His children. Therefore, he is the enemy of our victory.

The good thing is that we are *"not ignorant of his [Satan's] devices"* (2 Corinthians 2:11). We know that he will attack us and how he will do it, so we are able to build up our defenses against him.

If you knew that someone was intent on breaking down the front door of your house, coming in and killing you or your family members, you would do everything in your power to prevent it. You would put up some sort of barricade or reinforcement to keep the intruder out. The same must be done in the spiritual realm. Once we know how the devil works, we can build up a strong defense against him.

Satan attacks us in one of three ways (1 John 2:16):

1. *"The lust of the flesh"*
2. *"The lust of the eyes"*
3. *"The pride of life"*

The Bible tells us:

> *There hath no temptation taken you but such as is COMMON TO MAN: but God is faithful, who will not suffer you to be tempted above that ye are able; but will with the temptation also make a way to escape, that ye may be able to bear it.*   1 Corinthians 10:13

What does the word *"common"* mean in this verse? It means "ordinary, everyday, the same methods every time." It doesn't make any difference what you're going through at the moment, someone else has already gone through the same thing. We know Satan's tactics, and we know that his efforts are against every believer.

Three Points of Temptation

The Bible says of Jesus:

> *[He] was in all points tempted like as we are, yet without sin.* Hebrews 4:15

From the gospel accounts of the temptation of Jesus (Matthew 13, Mark 4 and Luke 8), we see that Jesus was tempted in three points:

1. He was tempted through *"the lust of the flesh."* (Satan told Jesus to command stones to become bread to satisfy His stomach.)
2. He was tempted through *"the lust of the eyes."* (Satan offered to give Jesus everything His eyes could see.)
3. He was tempted through *"the pride of life."* (Satan tempted Jesus to jump off the high place to prove to everyone that He was God.)

One of these methods is the one the devil will use against you. He may try to tempt you with *"the lust of the flesh"* by urging you to accept the popular philosophy: "If it feels good, do it!" This philosophy dominates modern life, and many Christians become caught up in this temptation. When they do, the devil destroys their victory by causing them to dwell on things that satisfy the desires of the flesh, while neglecting the more important (spiritual) aspects of life.

The devil may tempt you with *"the lust of the eyes."* As with Jesus, he may show you all the things you could acquire in the world. If he succeeds, you will be swallowed up by greed and miss God's best for your life.

The devil may tempt you with *"the pride of life."* He wants you to think you are important. He wants you to exult yourself and say, "Hey, everybody, look at me! I'm really somebody now!" If Satan can accomplish this, he can rob you of your intended blessing.

Trust God to help you to not be ignorant of the devil's devices and to know that the temptation that has overtaken you is *"common to man."* He has used these methods before. Others have overcome him, and you can too.

"More Than Conquerors" in Spite of Satan's Efforts

The Bible assures us that we have weapons that can protect us from Satan's every move:

For the weapons of our warfare are not carnal,
but mighty through God to the pulling down
of strong holds.   2 Corinthians 10:4

If you try to battle Satan without using the weapons God has given you, then you will not be able to conquer. If you have *"put on the whole armor of God,"* and you have your supernatural weapons ready, no enemy can destroy your victory.

So, although we have enemies, we can say with Paul, *"Thanks be unto God, which always causeth us to triumph in Christ." "This is the victory that overcomes the world, even our faith."*

God has given us *"all things that pertain unto life and godliness,"* so everything you need to live a victorious life here on Earth is available. Whatever it takes to make you an overcomer, to make you victorious, is at hand. God has given it to you so that you can stand against, or withstand, the enemy's temptations and onslaughts.

"The Whole Armor of God"

Most of the provision Paul spoke of in his letter to the Ephesians (Ephesians 6:10-18) was defensive. He spoke of only one offensive weapon — the Word of God:

> *And take ... the sword of the Spirit, which is*
> *the word of God.*   Ephesians 6:17

The only part of the body not covered by the full armor Paul described was the back. That's why we have no business turning and running from the devil. When you do that, he can shoot you in the back. Meet him head-on, and you're covered.

You have *"the breastplate of righteousness"* and the girdle of *"truth"* (Ephesians 6:14), the shoes of *"peace"* (verse 15), *"the shield of faith"* (verse 16) and *"the helmet of salvation"* (verse 17). You are ready to face the enemy and to be victorious in every moment, but don't ever forget your sword.

Each of the three times Satan came against Jesus with temptation, the Lord responded with this same weapon. He said, *"It is written"* (Luke 4:4, 8 and 10), and Satan had to back off. When the devil comes to tempt you, you can do the same. Use *"the sword of the Spirit"* against him by quoting the Word of God. Use the Word of God to pull down the strongholds of Satan and overcome his common, old, ordinary tactics against you.

We do have enemies, and we need to know how to recognize these enemies and their tactics and how to face them down with God's truths. Jesus summed it up when He said, concerning the devil:

> *The thief cometh not, but for to steal, and to kill, and to destroy: I am come that they might have life, and that they might have it more abundantly.* John 10:10

Satan's entire purpose is to steal from you the victory that God has given you. He wants to destroy your spiritual life. He will even kill you if he can. He will try to destroy your confidence in yourself and in God. He will try to destroy your family relationships. He will try to steal what God has put in your heart and life. Satan is your avowed enemy, and he will do everything he can to destroy you.

Now you know to expect Satan's attacks, you know that you don't have to be *"ignorant of his devices,"* and you know how to respond to him. Build up a strong wall of defense against every enemy with the mighty Word of God!

5

The Secret to Overcoming the Powers of Darkness

And you, being dead in your sins and the uncircumcision of your flesh, hath he quickened together with him, having forgiven you all trespasses; blotting out the handwriting of ordinances that was against us, which was contrary to us, and took it out of the way, nailing it to his cross; and having spoiled principalities and powers, he made a shew of them openly, triumphing over them in it. Colossians 2:13-15

Evil began with Satan. I like to ask people, "How do you spell the word *devil*?" When they answer, I say, "What would happen if you left off the *d*? You'd have *evil*, wouldn't you? " Evil is of the devil.

Satan is evil, and there is evil in the world because of him. He is the instigator of the whole process of evil in the Earth.

When God determined, before the foundation of the world, to send His Son Jesus into the world, it was with the purpose of overthrowing the devil and evil.

He did just that. Jesus came into the world and won the victory over death, Hell and the grave. He did it for you and me, so we have victory over the devil and all his works.

The secret to victory is not struggling to obtain something new, but resting in the victory that has already been given to us through Jesus Christ. We don't have to work to win the victory; we just need to rest in Jesus, for He has already done the work. The victory is won for us. God had our victory in His plans from before the creation of the world. He knew that we would have struggles and temptation, but His love and grace also planned our redemption and victory.

Jesus Came to Restore Victory and Dominion

We had no victory until Christ defeated Satan. When He did, He took away Satan's rights.

Adam had committed high treason in the Garden of Eden by transferring the power, dominion and authority of the Earth to Satan. God had given Adam dominion over everything on the Earth (see Genesis 1:26 and 28), but when Adam started listening to Satan, and when he and Eve ate the fruit from the tree of the knowledge of good and evil, his power was transferred to Satan (see 2 Corinthians 4:4).

We can condemn Eve all we want, but she was deceived. With Adam, however, it was a different story. He partook of the forbidden fruit with his eyes wide open. He was not deceived. He knew what he was doing. He had power and authority over the serpent and could have stopped the process if he had wanted to. What he did was high treason, and by it, he transferred his God-given power and authority to Satan.

The very first promise God ever gave to man was concerning Satan and our victory over him:

> *And I will put enmity between thee and the woman, and between thy seed and her seed; it shall bruise thy head, and thou shalt bruise his heel.*   Genesis 3:15

God was foretelling the coming of a Savior who would come to Earth to destroy the works of Satan. Now, many thousands of years later, we live on the other side of this promise. It was accomplished, and we are now living with the benefits of the cross.

Throughout the Bible, this word *"seed"* is used to denote offspring. These offspring, of course, are the fruit of man's seed. Here, however, God speaks of *"her seed."* Could a woman have "seed"? Not normally, but God was foretelling the coming of One who would be born of a woman without the natural process of conception. The seed would be implanted supernaturally in her by the power of God.

The One who would come forth from the woman without the natural process of conception, of course, would not be an ordinary man. Divinely implanted into the womb of the woman, He would be the very Son of God.

The writer of Hebrews declared:

> *Forasmuch then as the children are partakers of flesh and blood, he also himself likewise took part of the same; that through death he might destroy him that had the power of death, that is, the devil.*   Hebrews 2:14

Jesus Himself said:

> *Now is the judgment of this world: now shall the prince of this world be cast out.*
>   John 12:31

It is finished. Satan's power is destroyed. He can do only what you allow him to do. He has no other authority than the authority you give him.

When Jesus died on the cross, He took back those rights. Then, when He had risen from the dead, He was able to say to His disciples:

> *All power is given unto me in heaven and in earth.*   Matthew 28:18

And what did Jesus do with this power? He immediately transferred it to us: He said:

> *Go ye therefore, and teach all nations, baptizing them in the name of the Father, and of the Son, and of the Holy Ghost: teaching them to observe all things whatsoever I have commanded you: and, lo, I am with you alway, even unto the end of the world. Amen.*
> Matthew 28:19-20

Jesus was saying, "I give you My rights. I give you My power. I give you the authority that I took away from Satan. Now, *'go ... and teach all nations.'* "

With His sacrifice on the cross, Jesus wiped out man's sin and guilt, and He also took away Satan's rights and privileges. He effectively silenced *"the accuser of the brethren,"* and He did it as a man.

Jesus had to be tempted as Adam was tempted, but He did not have to yield to that temptation. He could resist and overcome the temptation, and in the process, He could provide a way of escape for us:

> *Now once in the end of the world hath he appeared to put away sin by the sacrifice of himself.*   Hebrews 9:26

Victory is already yours, yet you will not experience the victory that overcomes the world if you doubt that it's really yours. The only way to live in complete victory is to come to a place of full conviction and be able to say, "I have victory in Christ Jesus. I appropriate for myself the victory gained through the sacrifice of Jesus Christ. Therefore, I am an overcomer. Anything that comes against me, I will overcome it. I will be victorious. Nothing that is formed against me shall prosper. I shall always accomplish all that God intends for me to do."

> *For verily I say unto you, That whosoever shall say unto this mountain, Be thou removed, and be thou cast into the sea; and shall not doubt in his heart, but shall believe that those things which he saith shall come to pass; he shall have whatsoever he saith. Therefore I say unto you,*

What things soever ye desire, when ye pray,
believe that ye receive them, and ye shall have
them.   Mark 11:23-24

Resist Doubt, Guilt and Condemnation

Satan will try his best to cause you to doubt your
victory, to doubt what God has already done in your
life. He will probably not try to tempt you with some
flagrant temptation. Usually, he uses more subtle
methods of enticement.

He may take something good and cause it to become a problem for you. For example, although it is
healthy to be sorry for your sins, it is certainly not
healthy to continually dwell on them. Christ has
taken away your sins. Therefore, do not allow the
devil to make you constantly feel the guilt and pres-
sure of past sins. Christ paid the price for your sins:

Blotting out the handwriting of ordinances that
was against us, which was contrary to us, and
took it out of the way, nailing it to his cross.
                                 Colossians 2:14

Every sin you ever committed, every one of your
transgressions (all recorded in Heaven), was blotted out when you accepted Jesus Christ as your
Savior. After you have confessed your sin and been

forgiven, if you again feel guilty for what you did in the past, you can know immediately who is bringing those accusations against you. It's not God. He loves you, and He has blotted all those bad things from His memory.

God will never condemn you. If you are feeling condemned, that is Satan attempting to destroy your faith and take away your victory. If you were to go to God and ask Him to forgive you for the same thing you asked forgiveness for yesterday, He would say to you, "What are you talking about?" He has already forgotten (see Isaiah 43:25, Hebrews 8:12 and Hebrews 10:17).

Satan will constantly try to bring to your mind every mistake you have ever made. He loves to make you feel guilty about something in the past. Don't permit him to torment you with such thoughts. The work of the devil has no effect upon the life of a Christian who will boldly declare what God has done for him.

Declare:

> *There is therefore now no condemnation to them which are in Christ Jesus.*   Romans 8:1

When you do that, the devil can't stay around tormenting you, and your victory is assured.

The book of Revelation reveals the fact that Michael and his angels overcame the dragon and his angels (see Revelation 12:7-9). This victory was possible because of Christ's sacrifice and because of the testimony of the saints in Christ:

> *And they overcame him by the blood of the Lamb, and by the word of their testimony; and they loved not their lives unto the death.*
>
> Revelation 12:10-11

As a Christian, you will never know full and continuous victory in your life until you come to the place of knowing that you stand in the presence of God without guilt. You can accomplish it with the confession of your mouth, "I am victorious in Christ!"

When Satan brings guilt and condemnation to you, you can say, *"There is therefore now no condemnation to them which are in Christ Jesus."* You can say it because you received the blood of the Lamb when you accepted Jesus as your personal Savior. Through Jesus Christ, you entered into a blood covenant relationship with your Father, God. Now you can overcome *"by the blood of the Lamb, and by the word of [your] testimony."*

If you do as some people do, going around talking about how the devil has been after you and how he is attacking you, you will not be an overcomer. You will not experience victory. If, on the other hand, you testify, "I have been covered by the blood of the Lamb," you will be able to overcome the devil when he comes against you. You'll say to him, "There is no condemnation to them that are in Christ Jesus. Therefore I have victory. Thanks be unto God, who always causes us to triumph in Christ."

The last part of Revelation 12:11 declares:

And they loved not their lives unto the death.

These saints were obedient to the Scriptures, not thinking of themselves more highly than they ought. Pride and a haughty spirit opens a door to Satan and gives him something to work with. Be careful. If he lights the fuse, you might "blow up" inside.

Through Christ, Satan Has No Place in You

The victorious Christian must stand with Jesus when He said:

Hereafter I will not talk much with you: for the prince of this world cometh, and HATH NOTHING IN ME. John 14:30

The devil tried everything within his power to destroy Jesus. He tried planting thoughts in Jesus' mind through the murder of John the Baptist, Jesus' beloved cousin. He tried to get Jesus to open His heart to hatred against Herod for that vile act. However, Jesus refused to allow hatred to enter His spirit. He could confidently declare that Satan had nothing in Him.

There was no room in Jesus' heart for Satan, and He is our model. We, too, must be able to say that the devil has nothing in us. If Satan can find some weakness in us to work with, something like envy, ill will, unforgiveness toward someone, secret pride, unclean lust, prejudice or a desire for the praise of men more than the praise of God, he will try to exploit that weakness and use it to his advantage.

When Satan comes to us, can we say, as Jesus did, that the devil has nothing in us? We can. It's not a lie. It's true because of what God has done for us on the cross of Calvary. Jesus bore your sins on that tree, and since Jesus bore your sins, then you don't have them any longer (once you've accepted Him as Savior and you've asked Him to forgive you). Since Jesus took your sickness upon Himself, you don't have to receive or accept sickness. Jesus took your sicknesses for you on the tree.

Jesus bore our sins and carried our sicknesses so

that we could be free from sin, sickness and disease and live as overcomers. Some persons might ask, "Why, then, do I feel like I do?" Maybe it is because these individuals have not recognized what God has already done for them in carrying their sicknesses, as well as their sins.

A Summarization of Christ's Victory

I once shared this message with an attorney, and he summed up our victory in Christ in this statement:

> *We have received victory through Jesus Christ. It has already been given to us. It's already ours. Jesus can't do more for you than He's already done. God has already forgiven you of every sin. He has already healed you of every disease. He has already given you full victory. He has already made you an overcomer through Him. He has already given you power over all the power of the enemy. That's why, when Jesus died on the cross, His last words were, "It is finished." In other words, He was saying, "I can't do any more. I've done it all. Everything has been accomplished."*

If we are still not living in the victory God has already given us, it may be that we are somehow allowing Satan to steal or destroy our victory. This is not necessary. He has already been defeated.

When Jesus went into Hell, certainly He had already done everything that was demanded to redeem mankind. Still, He went further.

He shook off all the sins, all the diseases and all the afflictions of mankind, throwing them aside. Then He walked over to Satan, threw him down on the ground, placed His foot on Satan's neck and took from him the keys of death, Hell and the grave. Afterward, Jesus arose from that place triumphant and victorious. He ascended to the right hand of the Father, and He is there today, right now, interceding for you and me.

Friend, every sin you have ever committed has been forgiven. In reality, when Jesus consummated His great act of redemption, every sinner on the face of the Earth was forgiven of all sins. Every person who would ever be born was forgiven.

You might ask, "Then why is it that not everyone is forgiven? Why is it that not everyone is walking in that truth?" It is because they have not received the gift that God handed to them. They can have it. It belongs to them. They have victory over sin, guilt, condemnation, disease and death. They need only to choose to receive it. Now, death to a Christian is not the end of life. It is simply a transfer of existence.

This transfer can be compared to the birth of a baby. When it is time for a baby (who has been living inside his mother's womb) to be born, he struggles to come out. The mother suffers great pain, and, according to physicians, there is even a little hesitancy on the part of the baby to depart from the wonderful refuge that the womb has provided. That child has never experienced the world, and does not know what lies in store for him or her. Nothing can ultimately keep the baby back from being born without bringing great harm to either the child or the mother or both. That child is "destined" to be born.

In this same way, many Christians struggle with the issue of death because they're not sure exactly what's on the other side of their present existence. The unknown causes them concern. But we have nothing to be concerned about. We have victory. We have victory over everything. Nothing can hold us back unless we permit it. Satan's attempts against us will not prosper because we already have victory. It's ours. We are not destined for defeat.

Why should we struggle to obtain something that already belongs to us? God's Word shows us that salvation is already ours. If we have accepted Jesus as our Savior, sin has no rule over us. There's no need for us to feel guilty over past mistakes. Our trust is in the risen Savior, who conquered principalities and powers. We are risen with Him.

Jesus said:

> *I am Alpha and Omega, the beginning and the ending.*   Revelation 1:8

Many Christians ask, "Where do I fit in?" You fit right in the middle of Him. He is all around you. And God wants you to know this very important fact: You have victory in Christ!

Victory Through Obedience

Casting down imaginations, and every high thing that exalteth itself against the knowledge of God, and bringing into captivity every thought to the obedience of Christ.   2 Corinthians 10:5

Most Christians love to talk about victory. They love to hear teaching about the fact that Jesus paid the price for us and won our complete victory on the cross of Calvary. The fact that Jesus did everything and, therefore, we don't have to do anything but receive it is a pleasant thought to them. Many of these same Christians, however, don't like to hear about a very important aspect of our victory — the obedience it requires.

From the time we are small children, we don't like to hear about the need for obedience. Because of the sin nature, children are disobedient, and they stay that way until they accept Christ as Savior.

When our son Greg was just a little boy, we were trying to teach him to be obedient and not to bother things that didn't belong to him. One day we were at my grandmother's house. In her living room, she had a beautiful little porcelain bird on the coffee table, and Greg kept wanting to play with that fragile bird. We kept giving him a little smack on the hand and telling him "No," until finally Greg changed tactics.

He hadn't given up his desire to play with the bird, but he knew that we were watching him, so he did something different. This time, he didn't look at the bird at all, but kept his eyes away from it. At the same time, however, he began to back up toward the coffee table. When he bumped into the table, he put one hand behind him, and ever so slowly he began to walk his fingers over toward that little treasure. He wanted what he wanted, and it was hard for him to think that he couldn't have it.

As Greg grew up, he learned obedience and became a happy and well-behaved child, but that incident from his childhood always stuck in my mind.

Far too many Christians act just like Greg did when he wanted that bird. They want to be able to do what they want to do, without any strings attached, but the Christian life simply doesn't work that way.

We cannot have victory unless we are obedient to the faith, obedient to what God commands us to do. For example, if we want to have salvation, we cannot receive it any other way except through *"Jesus Christ and Him crucified"* (1 Corinthians 2:2 and Acts 4:12). Jesus said that if a man tries to come into the fold in any other way, *"he is a thief and a robber"* (John 10:1). You can't be saved any other way; you must become obedient to our Good Shepherd.

When God commands that something be done a certain way, then it has to be done that certain way. He is God. The basics for victorious Christian living are found in this verse from Paul's letter to the Galatians:

> *I live; yet not I, but Christ liveth in me.*
>   Galatians 2:20

When we come into submission to the authority of Almighty God to the degree that it is no longer "[us], but Christ ... in [us]," we can enjoy victory in our lives. As the popular Christian song goes, "It is no longer I that liveth, but Christ that liveth in me." If we don't have enough of the "it's-no-longer-I" attitude, then we will likely experience a lot of defeat in our lives.

Submit to God in Obedience

Because of his total commitment to God, Paul could say, *"I can do all things through Christ which strengtheneth me"* (Philippians 4:13). There was no "I" in him. There was no attitude of "Look at me; look what I can do; look who I am." It was Paul who said, *"I am crucified with Christ."* In other words, every part of Paul was surrendered and in obedience to Christ. He had brought every thought *"into captivity ... to the obedience of Christ"* (2 Corinthians 10:5). He had come to a point that "I" no longer ruled and reigned in his life. That's why Paul could say, *"I can do all things through Christ which strengtheneth me."*

The basic rule of Paul's life was, "Lord, what would You have me do?" It wasn't what Paul wanted to do. Therefore, when Paul did anything, it was done out of obedience to what God had told him to do.

It was because of this deep dedication to the Lord that Paul was so successful as a missionary and apostle. It was the reason that his ministry changed so many lives and established churches around the world. It was not Paul who was living and doing the works; it was Christ living in him.

Paul did whatever God told him to do. If God told him to go to Ephesus, Paul went to Ephesus. If God told Paul to go to Corinth, he went to Corinth. That's why, when Paul came to the end of his life, he could say:

> *I have fought a good fight, I have finished my course, I have kept the faith: henceforth there is laid up for me a crown of righteousness.*
> 2 Timothy 4:7-8

Because Paul was *"not disobedient unto the heavenly vision"* (Acts 26:19), he could stand before King Agrippa, Festus and the emperor in Rome and say, "I have not been disobedient to the commandments of my God."

Obedience = Victory
Disobedience = Defeat

The reason Paul was victorious in life, therefore, was the fact that he was *not* disobedient to God. When disobedience enters our lives, we quickly come to a point of defeat. The reason many people are defeated and are not living the overcoming life

is that they are not being obedient to what God has
told them to do.

Heed the Conditions of God's Promises

If we want the victory God offers, we must be obedient to Him. As we saw with the seven churches in
Chapter 3, a condition is usually attached to His
promises. If we meet that condition — if we obey
God — then no power of the devil can prevent us
from receiving the benefits and blessings of that particular promise.

One reason God has put conditions on His promises is that He did not want lazy Christians. He
requires that we do something in order to receive
the benefits of His promises. If some don't believe
that, they need only read Proverbs:

> *Go to the ant, thou sluggard; consider her ways,*
> *and be wise.*   Proverbs 6:6

The ant works all summer long to prepare for win-
ter, and we are instructed to learn from this small
but powerful creature. God is saying to us: "Do like
she does — work!"

Paul agreed with this principle. He wrote:

> *If any would not work, neither should he eat.*
>   2 Thessalonians 3:10

There are other scriptural passages that confirm this truth. God intends for us to do something to show our seriousness before He blesses us. He wants us active, not lazy.

When we meet the conditions of God's promises, we receive the benefits of His promises, and nothing and no one can prevent us from receiving them. Our acts of obedience assure our victory.

Set Apart for God's Service

Part of our obedience unto victory includes being sanctified, or set apart, for God's service. Many have a wrong concept of what it means to be sanctified.

Once, when my wife and I were eating in a certain restaurant, a man came up to us and said to me, "Brother, do you know the meaning of the word *sanctification*?"

I said, "Yes, sir, I sure do. It means 'set apart for the service of, dedicated for service.' "

He said, "Well, I want to tell you something. Your driving that nice car out there is not sanctification. It's not right for a preacher to drive a big luxury car like that. That is definitely not sanctification."

I said, "Wait a minute. That car is sanctified. It is set apart for the service of God, and it carries me around to do the Lord's work. That's what it's for. Besides that, I can give you scriptural evidence that it is good for me to drive a new car."

The man said, "Where does the Bible say that?"

I answered, "Do you remember where it says Jesus rode into Jerusalem in the great triumphal entry? I want you to notice that He did not send His disciples to get a broken-down old swayback nag for Him to ride. Jesus didn't find just any old donkey that no one wanted anymore. No, Jesus sent the disciples after a colt that no man had ever ridden. That's why I know that it's good for me to drive a new car."

The man sat down and didn't say another word. Sanctification is not so much about externals as it is about being dedicated to God's service, and it requires obedience on our part.

Make Jesus Lord of Your Whole Life

Most Christians have never crowned Christ as Lord of their lives. This accounts for the fact that they have also never learned to live victoriously. Christ must be Lord and Master of our lives before we qualify for His benefits. Some might insist that they have done it, but if they have, they have done it only with words, not with deeds. Declaring that Jesus is Lord of our lives is one thing. Living in the place of unquestioning and unhesitating obedience to Him is quite another. Living in victory requires a day-by-day, moment-by-moment life of full surrender in obedience to God.

F.B. Meyer, a great pioneer preacher of years gone by, once told about the way he obtained victory in his life. He said that after many years of living for the Lord, the Lord spoke to him one day and told him that he still needed to surrender one last "key" of his life.

"Don't hold back a single key to any door of your life," the Lord told him. "I want you to surrender them all."

F.B. Meyer responded, "Lord, I've done that."

"No," the Lord said to him, "there's one key that you have not yet surrendered." Still, Pastor Meyer was not sure what that key was.

Time went by — days, weeks, and then months — and the Lord continued to speak to Pastor Meyer to surrender some "last key." Each time, he responded, "Lord, I've given You all the keys."

Finally one day, it began to dawn on him what that final key was. It was a matter of obedience in his personal life that had to be reckoned with. The Lord required *all,* and he realized that he had held back something. He would have to surrender that final "key," and he did.

Meyer said, "When I gave the Lord that last key to the door of my life, I entered into a life of victory like I had never known before." Those who have read any of the works of F.B. Meyer know that he was one of the most mightily anointed men of God of this past century. He didn't reach that point until

he surrendered his own will to the obedience of
Christ.

If we, as Christians, want to enter into a life of
overcoming and experience the total and consistent
victory in our lives that He has promised, there is a
requirement. At some point, we will be required to
respond to the Lord's question of total surrender of
every part of our lives to Him. There is no other av-
enue to victory. Jesus must reign supreme over our
time, our finances, our thoughts and our words. He
must be Lord over our loved ones. He must be given
access to every fiber of our being and every facet of
our lives.

Every part of our lives must be brought into glorious submission to the obedience of God, for the
Lord lovingly whispers, "Obey Me. Obey Me." And
obedience brings the release of victory in our lives.

Once we come to the place of total submission and
surrender to God, we no longer need to seek after
victory. It becomes automatic.

Walk in God's Love, Grace and Victory

When you obey God, victory is inevitable. If you
are in total obedience to God, you can no more stop
victory than you can keep the Earth from turning
on its axis. And no one else can stop victory from
coming to you either.

When the love of God is instilled within your life

and you are obedient to the voice of the commandment of the Word of God, you can't stop victory. It
will flow out of your innermost being like rivers of
living water.

The primary commandment of God is that we
have faith in His Son and that we love one another:

> *And this is his commandment, That we should*
> *believe on the name of his Son Jesus Christ, and*
> *love one another, as he gave us commandment.*
> 1 John 3:23

With disobedience comes defeat, despondency
and fear. But those who are walking in total obedience to God don't get depressed. They are no longer
afraid (see 1 John 4:18).

If we are walking in God's love, then fear, depres-
sion and dejection will not have dominion over us.
Loving God and loving others combines all the commandments into one. We are to love as God loves,
and this perfect love will cast out every fear.

As we read the Bible, we cannot help but notice
that every time God told someone to do something
(and that person obeyed God's command), some mi-
raculous event took place, and victory came to the
child of God.

For example, when the children of Israel came to
the Red Sea, God told Moses what to do. When

Moses obeyed God, the sea rolled back, and the children of Israel walked across the sea on dry ground (see Exodus 14:21-22).

Scenes like this one were repeated over and over in the pages of the Bible. Whenever the children of Israel were obedient to God, they walked in victory. Whenever they committed any act of disobedience, defeat awaited them.

Defeat always comes with disobedience, so if you want victory, realize that victory is synonymous with obedience. Each of us must *"bring into captivity every thought to the obedience of Christ."* We have received the *"grace"* of God *"for obedience to the faith."*

What is *grace?* It is "the unmerited favor of God." Grace is much more than we have known it to be. It is really God's power and ability extended to us, and it comes when we decide to become obedient to the faith.

There is absolutely nothing Satan can do about my victory as long as I walk in obedience to the commandment of God's Word. There is not a devil in Hell that has power to drag me away from the love of God that is in Christ Jesus. I am the only one with power to relinquish it. I have the victory, and I am determined to keep the victory by walking in obedience to the commandment of God's Word.

Even angels, although they *"excel in strength,"* also *"hearken"* to God's commandments (Psalm 103:20).

I believe the very reason for the angels' excellence in strength is because of their obedience to the commandment of God's Word, and if we desire to excel in strength, we must also be obedient to the commandment of His Word.

The patriarchs and saints of old, from Abraham to Peter and beyond, became strong through obedience to God. They did mighty exploits, but not in their own strength.

> *Who through faith subdued kingdoms, wrought righteousness, obtained promises, stopped the mouths of lions, quenched the violence of fire, escaped the edge of the sword, out of weakness were made strong, waxed valiant in fight, turned to flight the armies of the aliens.*
>
> Hebrews 11:33-34

These mighty deeds were all done through faith. Through faith, these men and women became *"more than conquerors through Him who loved us."* Through our faith and obedience, we too can *"always triumph in Christ Jesus"!*

7

Encouraging Your Way to Victory

> *And David was greatly distressed; for the people spake of stoning him, because the soul of all the people was grieved, every man for his sons and for his daughters: but David encouraged himself in the LORD his God.*   1 Samuel 30:6

David had good reason to be distressed. I would be distressed too if people were about to stone me; wouldn't you?

David and his men had been away

in battle. While they were gone, an enemy band had come and captured the city where David and his men all lived. This band of enemies had taken captive all the women and children in the city, then plundered it and left it in ruins. When David and his men returned and saw what had happened, they were so stricken with grief that they sat and cried until they could cry no more.

In time, the men around David began to blame him for what had happened, and there was talk among them of stoning him to death.

So David was doubly distressed. He was distressed about what had happened to his family, and he was distressed about what was happening to his men. Suddenly, they wanted to kill him!

Many of us know what it is to have severe problems in life, and many of us have gone through distressing times and can identify with David. You may be going through a difficult time right now. The devil, our common enemy, may be trying his best to steal from you, to kill you and to destroy everything that God has done in your life. It is important, therefore, that we notice what David did in his time of grief: *"David encouraged himself in the Lord."*

David not only encouraged himself in the Lord; he also asked God what he should do in the situation:

*And David said to Abiathar the priest,
Ahimelech's son, I pray thee, bring me hither
the ephod. And Abiathar brought thither the
ephod to David. And David enquired at the
LORD, saying, Shall I pursue after this troop?
shall I overtake them? And he answered him,
Pursue: for thou shalt surely overtake them, and
without fail recover all.*   1 Samuel 30:7-8

God promised David complete recovery *"without
fail."*

God's Encouragement Brings Victory!

When David asked the Lord what to do, God told
him to go after the Amalekites and get back what
belonged to him. He did, and he was able to kill all
but four hundred of the enemy soldiers. Then, just
as the Lord had promised, he recovered his family
and all the goods the Amalekites had carried away.
The families and belongings of his men were recovered that day as well. Nothing was lost. To the
contrary, David and his men were able to carry away
much spoils from the tents and saddlebags of the
slain Amalekites.

What had begun as an extremely distressing and
discouraging situation became a great victory. And
it all happened because *"David encouraged himself in
the Lord."*

There is a great lesson here for all of us to learn. If, in the midst of our trials, we can encourage ourselves in the Lord, our situations will turn around just as David's did. We, too, will recover everything that seems to have been lost. Therefore, we would do well to learn what it means to encourage ourselves in the Lord.

A dictionary definition of the word *encourage* is "to inspire with courage, spirit, or hope; to stimulate." The meaning of the original Hebrew word, here translated as *encourage,* means "to be strengthened; to be built up and to fortify oneself." This is what we need to do, so *to encourage yourself* means "to be inspired with courage, spirit or hope; to be stimulated, strengthened, built up and fortified."

David started out right, of course, when he went to the Lord. Nothing could be more inspiring. When we turn to the Lord, He is always there, to stimulate, inspire and fortify us.

David knew where to turn, and you too must recognize your Source of help. If you turn to the wrong source, you will surely fail, but if you seek God in your distress and ask Him what to do, He will never fail you.

Don't Depend on Others for Your Victory

Too many times, we depend on other people to stimulate, inspire and fortify us, instead of looking to the Lord for His help. We expect too much of other humans. Although there are times that we will be inspired by the words others have for us, more often than not, we need to encourage ourselves as David did.

Paul's writings to the Ephesians help us to understand just how we can do this:

> *And be not drunk with wine, wherein is excess; but be filled with the Spirit; speaking to yourselves in psalms and hymns and spiritual songs, singing and making melody in your heart to the Lord; giving thanks always for all things unto God and the Father in the name of our Lord Jesus Christ.*   Ephesians 5:18-20

First, you must be able to build yourself up. Strengthen, or fortify, yourself by being filled with the Holy Ghost. Give yourself to Jesus Christ and let the Holy Spirit fill and saturate your life.

Next, you need to begin to speak to yourself. That's right — not to your neighbor, friend or fellow worker, but to yourself.

And what are we to speak to ourselves? *"Psalms and hymns and spiritual songs."* What is a *"psalm"*? We know it is one of the books of the Bible, but it means much more than that. The word, *"psalm,"* in Bible days meant "to be grateful, to express gratitude, to be joyful, to be filled with gladness, to make or to be merry, to give thanks," or "an expression of gratitude with a song or with music."

We are to speak to ourselves with expressions of gratitude and thanks to the Lord. We can do this in words, with a song, with an instrument, or with all of the above. A psalm is an expression of gratitude set to music, so if you get discouraged, just start singing, and you will feel a whole lot better.

Throughout the book of Psalms, we find that David and others made expressions of thanksgiving to the Lord in song again and again. In their psalms, we are constantly exhorted to worship the Lord and to do it not only with words and song, but also with musical instruments: psaltery, harp, lyre, organ, cymbals and drums. David used all of these means to build himself up.

Most of the psalms of praise we have in our Bibles were written by David at times when he was going through his greatest trials and battles. They were written at times when he was the most distressed. As we have seen, at one point, his friends were thinking of stoning him to death. Earlier in David's life, King Saul had been intent on killing him. It was in the midst of trials such as these that David encouraged himself with *"psalms, hymns, and spiritual songs, making melody in [his] heart to the Lord,"* and victory always came.

What does this word *hymn* mean? It means "to cel-
ebrate God in songs, to praise in a song." The
original word translated *"hymn"* comes from the
same root word from which we get our word *halle-
lujah.* So as we speak to ourselves in psalms (words
of gratitude set to music) and in hymns (celebrating
God in hallelujahs), great power is released.

The Bible goes even further when it exhorts us to
speak to ourselves *"in spiritual songs."* This phrase,
"spiritual songs," means "a manifestation of the ind-
welling Spirit of God." This is not just spirited or
animated singing. Rather, it is an actual song of the
Spirit.

There is a difference between spirited singing and
a song of the Spirit. Anybody can perform spirited
singing, but a song of the Spirit is unprepared, un-
premeditated and unlearned on your part. It flows
from your innermost being as a result of your being
filled with the Holy Spirit. It billows up from within
your soul. Let the Holy Spirit of God fill you to the
point that you begin to praise the Lord with a song
of praise in your heart, coming out of your lips, and
you will be encouraged.

The apostle Paul wrote:

> *What is it then? I will pray with the spirit, and
> I will pray with the understanding also: I will
> sing with the spirit, and I will sing with the
> understanding also.*   1 Corinthians 14:15

What was Paul saying? He was saying that because of the Holy Spirit within him, he could, as an act of his will, sing in the Spirit and allow the Holy Spirit to flow out through him. As an act of his will, he built himself up, fortified himself and encouraged himself by speaking the Word of God and *"singing psalms and hymns and spiritual songs."*

God Will Inhabit Your Praises

God has promised to inhabit the praises of His people (see Psalm 22:3). The word translated *"praises"* in this verse is the same word used for *"spiritual songs."* It means that the Lord inhabits our singing in the Holy Ghost. When we sing in the Holy Ghost, we can rest assured that the power of God rests, dwells in and inhabits our hearts and our lives.

After Paul wrote that we should be *"speaking to ourselves in psalms and hymns and spiritual songs,"* he said it again in another way: *"singing and making melody in your heart to the Lord."* He went on to say, *"Giving thanks always for all things unto God."* Thanksgiving is a big part of this encouragement process.

To the Colossians, Paul wrote:

> *Let the word of Christ dwell in you richly in all wisdom; teaching and admonishing one an-*

other in psalms and hymns and spiritual songs,
singing with grace in your hearts to the Lord.
                                        Colossians 3:16

We need to become melodious in our spirits.

Some may not feel like singing. They want to wait until they feel happy. But they need to begin to encourage themselves in the Lord right where they are, and then they will feel like singing.

Allow the Holy Spirit to flow in your life. Learn to teach and admonish others to do the same. With psalms and hymns and spiritual songs, with melody in your heart to the Lord, sing spiritual songs and scripture choruses, and you will be encouraged and established in your life of faith. When you sing the Word of God, it causes faith to build and grow and fill your heart.

There are still many people who believe that being happy and being a Christian are incompatible. Their concept of Christianity is that we must suffer, have problems, and live a life of sorrow. This could not be further from the truth of God's will. As Christians, we are to be merry. The Scriptures declare:

A merry heart doeth good like a medicine.
                                        Proverbs 17:22

What does medicine do? It is intended to bring

healing, to make you feel good again, to put some vim, vigor and vitality back into your life. So, if you want your spirit man to be healthy, start doing things that will make your heart merry. When it seems that everything is "caving in" around you, just start smiling and laughing. Begin to rejoice in the Lord. Begin to praise God and glorify Him from within yourself.

It is not always necessary to express your praise out loud, but it's much more effective if you can do it.

Praying in the Holy Ghost

Another thing we can do to build ourselves up is found in the little book of Jude:

> *But ye, beloved, building up yourselves on your*
> *most holy faith, praying in the Holy Ghost.*
> Jude 20

Praying in the Holy Ghost will cause your spiritual man to grow and to become stronger. If you want to live a victorious life, then pray in the Holy Ghost every day and speak to yourself in psalms, hymns and spiritual songs, giving thanks unto the Lord and making melody in your heart. As you do these things, you will grow quickly and stand very tall in the Lord. The victorious person is the one who encourages himself in the Lord.

When David was in the greatest distress of his life, he encouraged himself in the Lord. Many times you will not be able reach your best friend to pray with you. At times you won't be able to reach a minister and ask him to pray for you. So what are you to do? Encourage yourself in the Lord.

If you have been baptized with the Holy Spirit, then you have within you the ability to encourage yourself and to strengthen yourself in the Lord. This ability is yours; it belongs to you. Use it well, and you will find yourself walking in victory every day of your life.

The Possibility of Defeat

My little children, these things write I unto you, that ye sin not. And if any man sin, we have an advocate with the Father, Jesus Christ the righteous.   1 John 2:1

For Christ is not entered into the holy places made with hands, which are the figures of the true; but into heaven itself, now to appear in the presence of God for us.   Hebrews 9:24

I have been writing about the grace of the Lord extended to us and about the victory He has provided for us, but I would be remiss if I failed to mention the possibility of defeat.

God knows that we are human, so He has prepared for every eventuality. He has positioned Jesus to be our Advocate before Him. Jesus appears in the presence of God *"for us."*

When Jesus appears before the Father, it is not for His benefit, but for ours. He has not gone to Heaven to rest from His labors; He has gone to represent us.

Paul concurred with this truth in his letter to the Romans:

> *Who is he that condemneth? It is Christ that died, yea rather, that is risen again, who is even at the right hand of God, who also maketh intercession FOR US.*   Romans 8:34

He is not making intercession for only a handful, or for certain special people, but "for us," for every child of God.

God's Abundant Provision for Our Sins

Although the first letter of John to the churches does put forth the possibility of sin (*"if any man sin"*), it does not put forth the likelihood of defeat. Rather, it tells us that if we fail or make a mistake, God has made a provision for us: *"We have an advocate with the Father."* His name is Jesus.

John is not declaring the necessity to sin. He did not say, *"when* any man sins," but *"if* any man sin." We don't have to sin, but if we do, an abundant provision has been made for us that will allow us to continue to live in an unbroken state of victory. God has provided victory for us, not through our own perfection (for we have none in ourselves) but through Jesus Christ, for He is *"righteous."*

So even though we may fail, Paul's statement, *"Now thanks be unto God, which always causeth us to triumph in Christ,"* still stands. Because our victory depends on Him and He is perfect, we can triumph always despite our human weaknesses.

We can always live a victorious life, day in and day out, no matter what. The possibility of defeat is present, but our Advocate is ever ready to come to our defense. Failure is never a requirement, never a necessity, but when it happens, God knows how to handle it.

Many churches have taught so much about backsliding that some believers think that they must eventually backslide, that it is inevitable. This is wrong. We don't have to backslide, but even when we do make a mistake, God loves us, and His arms of forgiveness are open to us. He can cleanse us and help us to move on.

The fact that we are human does not alter or weaken in any way Paul's statement that we can always triumph in Christ. This is the miracle of it. We can triumph in spite of ourselves, because our victory is in Christ.

This is the divine side of the cross. It reveals that we *are* victorious — that we walk in victory, that we shall never fail, that we are always more than conquerors in all things, and that we have the unsearchable riches of Christ at our disposal. Praise God!

Human vs Divine

God's will for us is that we always have *"all sufficiency in all things."* The possibility of defeat has nothing to do with the divine side of our victory, which has already been established. I like to call it the "if" possibility of defeat, because the possibility of defeat has only to do with our human side of the equation, not the divine side.

God's will for us is clear. He wants us always to be in health and to prosper, even as our souls prosper. John wrote to the churches:

> *Beloved, I wish above all things that thou mayest prosper and be in health, even as thy soul prospereth.*   3 John 2

God's will is for us to have *"all sufficiency in all things"* so that we *"come behind in nothing"*:

> *And God is able to make all grace abound toward you; that ye, always having all sufficiency in all things, may abound to every good work.*
> 2 Corinthians 9:8

When we say, therefore, *"if any man sin,"* we are talking about the human element in the equation. Let me give you an example.

If you are a parent and your child gets sick, usually one of the first things you do is take him to a doctor. You don't *expect* your child to get sick, but if he does, you always do something to offset the sickness.

The normal state you expect in the child is not sickness. The normal state of a child is health. You expect your child to be robust and energetic. You expect to see him laughing, playing, romping, rolling, jumping up and down, and moving about constantly. If, in fact, your child is sitting down doing nothing, you might become concerned. That's not normal. If he is indeed sick (which is not the standard or norm), you do whatever is necessary to get him well again. You certainly don't abandon him.

The same is true of your spiritual life. If a Christian, even the most victorious Christian, should make a mistake and sin, that is not the norm. Concerning the normal Christian life, Paul wrote:

> *How shall we, that are dead to sin, live any*
> *longer therein?*   Romans 6:2

The norm for the Christian is to live a victorious, overcoming, robust, joyful spiritual life. God's standard for every Christian is victory. The robust, spiritual joy and overflowing love that emanates from the life of a born-again believer is the natural attitude, character and lifestyle that God intends for Christians.

So if a Christian does sin, it is because he has failed to take full possession of the provisions that are already his through Jesus Christ. If we fail as Christians, it doesn't mean that God's provision is not great enough. Rather, it means that we do not know how to take advantage of that provision, and consequently, we may suffer defeat before the onslaught of the world and the enemy.

Spiritual Growth and "Preventive Medicine"

If we do not take precautionary measures, we may find ourselves in a defeated position. We need some "preventive medicine." In the natural, there are vaccines that keep us from suffering the devastating effects of smallpox, polio and many other diseases, and the same is true in the spiritual. We must learn to take preventive measures that will keep us from ever having to know the agony of sin and defeat.

Once you have attained to a victorious state, it does not mean that you will never again have to face a battle or a problem. Living in victory does not mean that you can just sit back in ease and say, "I have arrived. I can just take it easy from now on." Of course not. We will all face battles in the future. The devil will throw everything he has against you and try his best to destroy you. He will attack you on every possible front.

The more you grow spiritually, the greater the attacks Satan will launch against you. Where there is an increased power of God, there will also be an increased power of Satan to try to combat what God is doing in your life. God will give you grace to withstand every attack.

God's Abounding Grace

We know Paul's secret: *"Thanks be unto God, which always causeth us to triumph in Christ"* (2 Corinthians 2:14). Paul also wrote:

> *Where sin abounded, grace did much more abound.*   Romans 5:20

When we see a wave of sin moving rampantly across the world and are tempted to think how terrible things are, we need to realize that, regardless of all Satan's destructive maneuvers, a great and mighty move of God is taking place at the same time. And God's people will always be victorious.

The 1960s was called the decade of drugs and the occult, for these practices became common during those years. Still, despite all the drug abuse and the illicit sexual practices of the period, a mighty move of God was felt in many circles, especially among the young people. Great numbers came to Christ. They called themselves the "Jesus People," and they went around the country declaring that Jesus was Lord and winning other young people to Him. Tens of thousands were delivered from drugs and promiscuity and brought out of darkness and into everlasting life with Jesus Christ. Anytime sin abounds, grace abounds much more. Where there is a problem, you will find always find a solution through Jesus Christ.

Prayer: The Key to Maintaining Victory

To maintain constant victory, we must *"watch and pray,"* as Jesus taught:

> *Watch and pray, that ye enter not into*

temptation: the spirit indeed is willing, but the
flesh is weak. Matthew 26:41

This is something that we must get into the habit
of doing every day of our lives. Through prayer, we
keep Jesus as the center of our spiritual lives. This is
vital, for He is our Source of victory. We receive our
salvation, our spiritual lives, and our overcoming
faith through Him. Everything we need is centered
in, around and through Jesus, the Christ. Outside of
Him, we have nothing.

He was "representative man." Everything that He
did, we did. Everything that He accomplished, we
accomplished. Everything Jesus was victorious over,
we became victorious over. As Paul said:

I am crucified with Christ: nevertheless I live;
yet not I, but Christ liveth in me.
Galatians 2:20

In another place, he said:

We have this treasure in earthen vessels, that
the excellency of the power may be of God, and
not of us. 2 Corinthians 4:7

"As He Is, So Are We"

What is this *"treasure"* Paul was speaking of? He

is talking about the life of Jesus within us. Jesus was an overcomer; He did not sin. He lived a victorious life, and since Jesus lived a victorious life, we live a victorious life. For *"as He is, so are we in this world"* (1 John 4:17).

How is Jesus? He is healthy, and because He is healthy, then so are we.

How is Jesus? He is prosperous, and because He is prosperous, then so are we.

How is Jesus? He is blessed, and because He is blessed, then so are we.

As He is, so am I. This is not something that I am making up; this is something that God's Word declares to be true.

So there is no possibility of defeat on the divine side. On the human side, however, there is the "if" possibility. In other words, we have a part to play in determining whether we live in victory or defeat.

One problem, on the human side, that lurks right around the corner from victory is the problem of pride. Pride says, "I can handle this myself." Even when God gets us out of a problem situation, there is a tendency to think, *Well, I can take care of everything now. Lord, You got me out of trouble, but I can take it from here. I can handle it myself now.* Then we go on about our business, trying to handle things ourselves, and inevitably, we "fall flat on our faces" and cry, "Oh, Lord, help!" Jesus then comes and gets us out of trouble again, and we turn around and say, "Thanks, Lord. I can handle it from here."

We go along in life, trying to accomplish things in our own ability, until we fail, and then we call on the Lord for help to get us out of a problem. This should not be. We should be living every day with Him as the center of our lives. He must be central in our thoughts and in all that we do.

Paul told the Romans:

> *Knowing this, that our old man is crucified with him, that the body of sin might be destroyed, that henceforth we should not serve sin.*
>
> Romans 6:6

To the Colossians, he said:

> *Mortify therefore your members which are upon the earth.* Colossians 3:5

What *"members"* was Paul talking about? He was talking about our own bodies. We must kill, destroy, *"mortify,"* the old fleshly desires. He went on to name some of them: *"fornication, uncleanness, inordinate affection, evil concupiscence, and covetousness, which is idolatry"* (Colossians 3:5).

A few verses earlier, Paul had declared:

> *For ye are dead, and your life is hid with Christ*
> *in God.*   Colossians 3:3

So, is this a contradiction? Not at all. Even though you are dead in your sins and your life is hidden with Christ in God, you must still mortify the members of your flesh. You must still die to sin and the things of the world. Even though you are a born-again child of God, you must keep the desires of your flesh under so that you can avoid defeat and disaster.

Dying Daily and Living in Continuous, Uninterrupted Victory

Paul practiced what he preached. He said that he died daily (1 Corinthians 15:31) and that he kept his body under subjection (1 Corinthians 9:27). We must do likewise if we aspire to an uninterrupted life of victory that never knows defeat.

My experience is that many Christians, when they have tried to live for the Lord and have made a mistake, get all upset in their spirits. *Oh, boy, I've blown it now,* they think. *I've sinned; I've gone back on God. Now He won't love me, and He won't answer my prayers. I might as well give up. I can't make it. I've tried before, and I've failed. Now I've done it again. I might as well quit.*

I've seen far too many people living under constant guilt and condemnation because of one mistake. What they should have done was to immediately say, "God, forgive me. I'm sorry for my mistake." The instant you sincerely ask for forgiveness, your sin is wiped out, and joy should return to your heart. Your sin will never be remembered against you again. It is immediately cleared, and you will have victory in Christ Jesus.

Don't allow Satan to make you think that you can't make it just because you have tried before and failed. Get up and go forward again. Before long, you'll reach a place where your victory is continuous and unbroken. Love never fails, and if we will walk in love, we will never fail. As you grow in the Lord, you can reach a point where you will not fail, so keep going. You're growing. You're getting there. Don't give up.

There is something else we can do to avoid defeat:

> *Beloved, believe not every spirit, but try the spirits whether they are of God: because many false prophets are gone out into the world.*
>
> 1 John 4:1

John was writing to victorious Christians, but he was telling them to *"try the spirits,"* to see whether or not they were of God. God was saying to us through John: "Check them out." Don't accept everything as coming from God. There are many false religions and teachings in the world, and we must not believe everything that we hear or everything we are told — even when people are using the name of Jesus. Many of those who use His name do not even know Him.

Jesus warned that in the last days there would be many false prophets. If something we hear is not backed up by the Word of God, we don't have to accept it.

No Longer Sinners, but Saints

Many Christians still see themselves as poor, miserable sinners, saved by grace. But if you have been saved by grace, then you're not a poor, miserable sinner any longer. You're a child of God. His royal blood flows through your veins.

Many constantly talk about how bad they are and how bad everything and everybody else is. They constantly live in that negative realm, when they should be obeying Paul's admonition:

> *There is therefore now no condemnation to them which are in Christ Jesus, who walk not after the flesh, but after the Spirit.*   Romans 8:1

As a Christian, you don't have to be defeated in life. If you do sin, then call on your Advocate with the Father, *"Jesus Christ the righteous."* He is *"ever living to make intercession for [you]."*

Say to Him, "Jesus, I come to You, and I ask You to forgive me."

He will turn to His Father and say, "Father, [insert your name here] is trusting in My blood and what I did for him/her on the cross. Wipe that sin from his/her record." Then, because of what Jesus has already done for you, your sin will be removed from your record and forgotten.

The Continual Cleansing Process

If you do become defeated, immediately ask God to forgive you. Then get back on the right side of God through Jesus Christ and start living the overcoming, victorious life again.

John wrote:

> *And these things write we unto you, that your joy may be full. This then is the message which we have heard of him, and declare unto you, that God is light, and in him is no darkness at all. If we say that we have fellowship with him, and walk in darkness, we lie, and do not the truth: but if we walk in the light, as he is in the light, we have fellowship one with another, and the blood of Jesus Christ his Son cleanseth us from all sin.*   1 John 1:4-7

In the original Greek, the word used for *"cleanseth"* here is in the present active tense. Therefore, this promise means, "The blood of Jesus Christ His Son *is continuously cleansing* us from all sin." He is continuously cleansing us — always, every day, twenty-four hours a day, sixty minutes of every hour, and sixty seconds of every minute. If any man sins, he has an Advocate with the Father who is continuously cleansing him.

The blood of Jesus is constantly in the process of cleansing us from all sin. When it seems as though you are about to be wiped out, go to the Father through Jesus Christ. He is in the process right then of talking to the Father about cleansing you because of His active, cleansing blood that is always working on your behalf.

Again, I want to emphasize, don't use this teaching as an excuse to sin. John did not say, *"when* you sin"; he said, *"if* you sin." It is not necessary to sin, but Jesus is there to intercede for you if you do.

The Possibility of Defeat Through Sickness

We can take this same principle and apply it in many different areas. James wrote concerning healing. He asked, *"Is any sick among you?"*

> *Is any sick among you? let him call for the elders of the church; and let them pray over him,*

anointing him with oil in the name of the Lord: and the prayer of faith shall save the sick, and the Lord shall raise him up; and if he have committed sins, they shall be forgiven him.

James 5:14-15

Provision is made for the possibility of sickness as well as sin, but you don't have to live in either sickness *or* sin. If you are sick, then call for the elders of the church. If you sin, then call on your Father God through Jesus Christ. Again, sin and sickness are not the norm, but if they do occur, then there is a way to get out of trouble.

Say, "Father, in Jesus' name, I'm sorry. Forgive me through Jesus' blood. I accept that blood, which is even now in the process of cleansing me — continuously, all the time." Then you'll immediately be back on the victory side because you are trusting in the ever-cleansing blood of Jesus Christ, God's Son.

Victory Through Death

For we would not, brethren, have you ignorant of our trouble which came to us in Asia, that we were pressed out of measure, above strength, insomuch that we despaired even of life: but we had the sentence of death in ourselves, that we should not trust in ourselves, but in God which raiseth the dead: who delivered us from so great a death, and doth deliver: in whom we trust that he will yet deliver us.

2 Corinthians 1:8-10

132

A great trial had come to the apostle Paul in Asia. What he experienced was apparently a process of death and resurrection. He had *"despaired even of life."* He emerged from the experience victorious, saying that he had been delivered from death, was being delivered from death, and was trusting God to deliver him from death in the future.

Here was a man who had identified himself closely with Jesus Christ the Savior in His death and resurrection. He said: *"I am crucified with Christ"* (Galatians 2:20), *"I am dead to sin"* (see Romans 6:2, 10-11 and 13), *"I am resurrected with him"* (see Romans 6:4, Ephesians 2:6 and Colossians 2:12), and *"I have been made to sit in heavenly places with him"* (see Ephesians 2:6).

Paul spoke much of our identification with Christ. As we have seen, when Jesus died as the Son of Man, He died as the representative of all people. Paul said that our old man was crucified with Jesus, buried with Him, and raised into newness of life in Him.

His experience in Asia proved the things he had been teaching for so long. The great trial that came to his life resulted in victory through death.

Paul was so distressed at one point that he said, *"We were pressed out of measure and had the sentence of death in ourselves."* In essence, he was saying, "What do I have to fear? Have I not already died to the world? Have I not already been crucified? Have I not already tasted this death?" Paul was coming into a relationship with the Savior to the point that he could say, "Jesus died; and I have already died with Him. So if I am pressed out of measure, even to the point of death, should it bother me? Is not my life already hid with Christ? Am I not already given into His keeping?"

Paul was saying that he had already experienced the world's worst. He was saying that he had already experienced the devil's utmost, his "best shot."

Some might ask, "How could that be? Paul was still living when he said that, and Satan might have tried to 'shoot' something else at him."

Identified With Christ

But Paul was identifying with Jesus Christ. Satan had already taken his best shot at the apostle when he tried to kill Jesus on the cross of Calvary. Satan had already done the worst that he could possibly do. Paul identified himself with Jesus on the cross, which meant that no matter what else Satan tried, he had already done his worst and lost. Jesus had already taken authority over Satan, conquered him and made Himself victorious. And, when He did that, He made us victorious too. We are victorious through Him.

Paul even said that to be *"absent from the body"* was to be *"present with the Lord"* (2 Corinthians 5:8). Paul was simply saying, "Listen, I am pressed on every side to the point that I even despair of life. It looks like I am about to die right now. Everything that could happen has happened. My life is ebbing out of my body. But I let it go, because if I leave this world, I reach into the fullness of all that God has for me in the heavenly life that will be mine someday." To the Christian, death is not a dreadful thought.

Please don't misunderstand what I am saying here. I am not saying that we should wish to die, and Paul was not expressing that desire either. He was merely expressing that he was not afraid to die if it was time for him to *"depart and be present with the Lord."* Paul believed that God's divine purpose was being fulfilled in his life and that if it was his time to die, it was okay because he knew he would be in Heaven with Jesus.

Paul also considered that if it was *not* his time to die, that was all right too. He knew that Satan had already done the worst he could do. No matter what else happened, Paul knew that he would come out of the situation victorious. Why? Because he said that God *had* delivered him, God *was* delivering him, and God *would* deliver him. Paul knew that he had the victory. It was already his. And Paul was convinced that Satan could not steal his victory.

Here in this passage (2 Corinthians 1), we have some very real principles for the Christian life. We cannot live a victorious life without dying to self and the world and coming alive unto Christ. Again and again in life, we will no doubt find ourselves in circumstances that will seemingly nearly "destroy" us — circumstances that will seem to offer no hope whatsoever. It will seem that there is no way out. Situations will develop that will seem to indicate that we just cannot make it, that we are about to be defeated. As defeat will stand before us and stare us in the eyes, it will say, "See there, I've got you this time. You cannot win. This is the end for you."

It is very important for us to praise the Lord in these circumstances, and the reason it's so important is that by praising the Lord we are showing that we are not trusting in our circumstances, but we're trusting in God. We're trusting in the One who Paul said *"raiseth the dead."*

Paul was ready to die. "If I die," he was saying, "so what? I put my trust in the One who raises the dead. If they kill me, so what? God will raise me back to life."

No one can do more to you than was already done to Jesus. They mocked Him, they spit on Him, they struck Him and they crucified Him, but God raised Him from the dead. Paul was saying, therefore, "If I put my trust in the Lord and identify with Him —

and I am doing just that — then I will constantly live in victory — no matter what happens."

Victory Through the Resurrection Power of God

The same power that raised Jesus from the dead will also work in *your* life in this way if you trust Him. The Bible says:

> *But if the Spirit of him that raised up Jesus from the dead dwell in you, he that raised up Christ from the dead shall also quicken your mortal bodies by his Spirit that dwelleth in you.*
>
> Romans 8:11

Paul wrote this epistle to the Romans under the inspiration of the Holy Ghost. In this particular verse, he was talking about being *"quickened,"* not just on Resurrection Day or when the Rapture takes place, but right now. God wants you to have victory right now — today. He has done everything within His power to provide victory for you. In fact, the power that operated in Jesus when He was raised from the dead is the same power that is available to your life today. The power that enabled Jesus to throw off the weight of the guilt of all the sins of the world and to snatch the keys of death, Hell and the grave from Satan is the same power that will work effectually in your life. Therefore, your answer can be the same as Paul's: "I am putting my trust in the Christ who raises the dead."

Hidden With Christ

In a moment-by-moment participation in the lifestyle of Christ, we are coming to the place of being what God wants us to be. Again, Paul wrote:

> *For ye are dead, and your life is hid with Christ in God.*   Colossians 3:3

Everything that could be said and done concerning our victory has already been said and done, and now nothing, by any means, will hurt or destroy us if we will walk in the light of the victory that God has provided for us.

Reckon yourself dead with Christ and risen together with Him, and you can be an overcomer. All the devils in Hell cannot take away from you the victory that God has given you, and angels certainly won't try to take it from you. So, nothing can disturb your victory. You have it. Proceed on this basis, living on this "resurrection ground," and it will make all the difference in your life.

Job's Victory Through Death

A good example is found in the book of Job. It was not until Job came to embrace this "death-and-resurrection" attitude that God really was able to bring deliverance to his life.

Job was miserable. He was covered with boils all over his body, he had lost all of his possessions, his wife had turned against him, and three of his good friends had come to accuse him rather than encourage him. At first, Job tried to defend himself to his friends. He knew that he loved God, and he said (in so many words), "Hey, don't tell me I'm a sinner. My record is in Heaven. I know where I stand."

It was true. Job was innocent. He was not a sinner, and that's why the accusations of his friends hurt so much. He knew he was doing the right thing, and they were accusing him of sin. They were blaming him for all the bad things that had happened in his life, when he knew that these things were not his fault.

In the end, Job prayed for these friends who were accusing him, and when he began to pray for them, things turned around for him as well:

> *And the LORD turned the captivity of Job, when he prayed for his friends: also the LORD gave Job twice as much as he had before.*
>
> Job 42:10

A hypothetical situation illustrates well this "victory-through-death" principle. Let's say, for example, that I've gotten my feelings hurt. Someone has slighted me and treated me badly. Someone has been inconsiderate of my feelings and has not given me the respect I deserved. My opinion was not taken into account, and I am offended by it.

Now in a case like this, I have done nothing wrong. The fault lies in others. Because my feelings have been hurt, however, the joy that usually causes me to smile is gone. The sparkle is gone from my eyes, and on my face, one can read hurt and disappointment.

Defeat soon begins to engulf me. I am devastated by something that is not my fault. Therefore, I cannot smile. I cannot sing. I can't even go to church. I am allowing defeat to completely overwhelm and overcome me because I am offended.

It should not be difficult for most of us to get this picture, because it has happened to us over and over again throughout our lives. Most of us have been there. We've felt totally crushed, misused and abused — emotionally wrung out and not good for much.

Think about it. How different our lives would be if, in moments like this, our thoughts were something like this: *Well, they crucified Jesus. What these people are doing to me is **nothing** compared to that. This is my chance to go a little bit deeper into the things of*

God and into the fellowship of my Savior. This is my opportunity to go deeper into the very sufferings of Jesus Himself and to be made conformable unto His image, to be made conformable to His suffering, His death, and His resurrection. Praise God that I am crucified with Christ and risen with Him.

If we had *that* kind of attitude, the result would be a fuller participation in the resurrection life of Jesus Christ. Instead of saying how hurt we were at what others had done to us, we could have said, like Jesus: "Father, forgive them, for they don't know what they're doing." This would have changed everything.

If we would have said, "Lord Jesus, I forgive them, even as You forgave. I'm hurt, but I'm also deeply grateful, Lord, that You have given me the opportunity to be made conformable to Your life, Your suffering, Your death and Your resurrection. You can now live Your life through me in such a way that those people who misused me and hurt my feelings will see You in me and see the positive change that has taken place as a result of this — then we would have experienced the power of the overcoming believer.

Don't Allow Offenses to Destroy You and Rob You of Victory

The battles that threaten your very life, the ones

that take every ounce of your strength to be able to stand, usually are not the battles that destroy you. In an obvious battle against evil, the devil will not be able to deceive you and cause you to sin. Some temptations, however, are not so obvious, and, quite possibly, more Christians have been destroyed over hurt feelings than over anything else.

I once met a man who, when he was a teenager, had his feelings hurt. He was raised in a Christian home, and his dad was a preacher, but after he had gotten his feelings hurt, he refused to accept Jesus Christ as his Savior and live for Him. Until the day he died, he refused to go to church and make things right with God. He could quote scripture as well as anyone I knew, yet because of the hurt he had suffered at the hands of Christians, he would not yield his life to the Lord. What a tragedy!

Again, I think that offenses and hurt feelings can do more to destroy the fiber of a Christian than just about anything else. We can easily be destroyed by such experiences if we do not learn the secret of victory through death, of victory through dying to self and letting Christ live through us.

Such defeat is unnecessary. Through identifying with Christ in His death, we can immediately turn every offense into something good in our lives. We can take every difficult situation and make it become something beautiful. The ugly things in our lives can become beautiful, and the bad things that happen to us can become good if we can only say, "I have died with Christ; therefore, I live with Him."

You will be surprised what operating in this principle will do in your home, in your job, in your church, among your friends, and particularly among your enemies. It may seem that the devil has you pinned with your back against the wall and is ready to thrust his dagger into your chest and put an end to your life. However, when all these things begin to happen, that's the time to sing. That's the time to encourage yourself in the Lord. Let the Holy Spirit begin to rise up within you. Then, instead of saying, "Oh, my, look at all the terrible things that are happening all around me," you can start saying with Job:

For I know that my redeemer liveth.
Job 19:25

And because He lives, we shall live also. This is our victory. *Angels Won't and Devils Can't* take it from you.

Nay, in all these things we are more than conquerors through him that loved us. For I am persuaded, that neither death, nor life, nor angels, nor principalities, nor powers, nor things present, nor things to come, nor height, nor depth, nor any other creature, shall be able to separate us from the love of God, which is in Christ Jesus our Lord.

Romans 8:37-39

Ministry address:

Arman Stephens
P.O. Box 970
Bethany, OK 73008

pastorarman@msn.com